NEW DIRECTIONS FOR EVALUATION
A Publication of the American Evaluation Association

Gary T. Henry, *Georgia State University*
COEDITOR-IN-CHIEF

Jennifer C. Greene, *Cornell University*
COEDITOR-IN-CHIEF

# Understanding and Practicing Participatory Evaluation

Elizabeth Whitmore
*Carleton University*

EDITOR

Number 80, Winter 1998

JOSSEY-BASS PUBLISHERS
San Francisco

UNDERSTANDING AND PRACTICING PARTICIPATORY EVALUATION
*Elizabeth Whitmore* (ed.)
New Directions for Evaluation, no. 80
*Jennifer C. Greene, Gary T. Henry,* Coeditors-in-Chief

Microfilm copies of issues and articles are available in 16mm and 35mm, as well as microfiche in 105mm, through University Microfilms Inc., 300 North Zeeb Road, Ann Arbor, Michigan 48106-1346.

*New Directions for Evaluation* is indexed in Contents Pages in Education, Higher Education Abstracts, and Sociological Abstracts.

ISSN 1097-6736          ISBN 0-7879-1553-X

NEW DIRECTIONS FOR EVALUATION is part of The Jossey-Bass Education Series and is published quarterly by Jossey-Bass Inc., Publishers, 350 Sansome Street, San Francisco, California 94104-1342.

SUBSCRIPTIONS cost $65.00 for individuals and $115.00 for institutions, agencies, and libraries. Prices subject to change.

EDITORIAL CORRESPONDENCE should be addressed to the Coeditors-in-Chief, Jennifer C. Greene, Department of Policy Analysis and Management, MVR Hall, Cornell University, Ithaca, NY 14853-4401, or Gary T. Henry, School of Policy Studies, Georgia State University, P.O. Box 4039, Atlanta, GA 30302-4039.

Cover design by Design Office.

www.josseybass.com

Printed in the United States of America on acid-free recycled paper containing 100 percent recovered waste paper, of which at least 20 percent is postconsumer waste.

## EDITORIAL POLICY AND PROCEDURES

*New Directions for Evaluation,* a quarterly sourcebook, is an official publication of the American Evaluation Association. The journal publishes empirical, methodological, and theoretical works on all aspects of evaluation. A reflective approach to evaluation is an essential strand to be woven through every volume. The editors encourage volumes that have one of three foci: (1) craft volumes that present approaches, methods, or techniques that can be applied in evaluation practice, such as the use of templates, case studies, or survey research; (2) professional issue volumes that present issues of import for the field of evaluation, such as utilization of evaluation or locus of evaluation capacity; (3) societal issue volumes that draw out the implications of intellectual, social, or cultural developments for the field of evaluation, such as the women's movement, communitarianism, or multiculturalism. A wide range of substantive domains is appropriate for New Directions for Evaluation; however, the domains must be of interest to a large audience within the field of evaluation. We encourage a diversity of perspectives and experiences within each volume, as well as creative bridges between evaluation and other sectors of our collective lives.

The editors do not consider or publish unsolicited single manuscripts. Each issue of the journal is devoted to a single topic, with contributions solicited, organized, reviewed, and edited by a guest editor. Issues may take any of several forms, such as a series of related chapters, a debate, or a long article followed by brief critical commentaries. In all cases, the proposals must follow a specific format, which can be obtained from the editor-in-chief. These proposals are sent to members of the editorial board and to relevant substantive experts for peer review. The process may result in acceptance, a recommendation to revise and resubmit, or rejection. However, the editors are committed to working constructively with potential guest editors to help them develop acceptable proposals.

Jennifer C. Greene, Coeditor-in-Chief
Department of Policy Analysis and Management
MVR Hall
Cornell University
Ithaca, NY 14853–4401
e-mail: jcg8@cornell.edu

Gary T. Henry, Coeditor-in-Chief
School of Policy Studies
Georgia State University
P.O. Box 4039
Atlanta, GA 30302–4039
e-mail: gthenry@gsu.edu

# CONTENTS

Zones/Enterprise Communities program. The authors describe the project and examine some of the lessons learned in doing transformative participatory evaluations at a macro level.

Three questions are explored: To what extent are the three dimensions of participation described in Chapter One present in practice? Are the two types of participatory evaluation—P-PE and T-PE—different in important ways in practice? And what has been learned from the case examples about implementing participatory evaluation?

# EDITOR'S NOTES

Participation is viewed generally as a positive activity, certainly in the context of democratic societies. Although still contested in some quarters, the idea of stakeholder participation in evaluation is now widely accepted within the evaluation community. Yet the meanings, even the purposes, of stakeholder participation in evaluation remain diverse, multiple, and thus clouded in many contexts. Many funding agencies, for example, are increasingly calling for "participatory evaluations" under the assumption that stakeholder participation will improve the quality of the evaluation results. Growing evidence indicates that this is indeed the case, but only in certain circumstances and only when the definition of "results" is clearly understood and agreed on by all parties. A comprehensive discussion of participation in evaluation, which is initiated in this volume, can help differentiate and clarify these kinds of issues.

The main purpose of this volume is to present participatory evaluation (PE) as a viable and creative addition to the contemporary repertoire of evaluation approaches. The volume addresses three basic questions: what is PE, under what circumstances is it most useful, and how does one actually do it in practice. The two primary themes in the volume are what we identify as the principal streams in PE: practical participatory evaluation (P-PE), which is pragmatic and has as its central function the fostering of evaluation use; and transformative participatory evaluation (T-PE), which is based in emancipation and social-justice activism and focuses on the empowerment of oppressed groups. These streams have emerged from quite different historical and ideological roots, a second important theme. A third theme positions PE more as a process of engagement than as a fixed set of technical methods. Within this process, however, some key "moments in implementation" and some clear how-tos can helpfully guide the evaluator. Finally, there are the challenges of putting PE into practice, including who should participate, technical quality, objectivity and bias, resources (especially time), ownership of results, and differing evaluator roles.

Chapter One presents the conceptual framework for the discussion. The authors, J. Bradley Cousins and Elizabeth Whitmore, identify and explicate the two PE streams and then compare them on three key dimensions: control of the evaluation process, stakeholder selection, and depth of participation. Control can be exercised entirely by the evaluator, at one end of this continuum, or by practitioners, at the other end. Stakeholder selection can be limited to primary users or include all legitimate groups. Depth of stakeholder participation can range from consultation to full involvement. The authors then situate PE in relation to other forms of collaborative evaluation, and collaborative inquiry.

Chapter Two addresses the history of PE and current debates in the field. The author, Sharon Brisolara, explores the differing historical and ideological roots of P-PE and T-PE in depth. She then examines a number of key issues in participation and evaluation and traces them in each stream.

In Chapter Three, the discussion of methodology begins with a set of PE principles, followed by key elements of the process that ensure the principles are carried through in the evaluation methodology. There is no easy-to-follow formula for conducting PE. Rather, Beverley Burke draws on her own experience, as well as the literature, to highlight "key moments and decisions" in the evaluation process; collectively these key decisions form a useful and detailed guide for the practitioner to use amid the dynamic, ongoing, evolving interaction among participants.

Chapters Four through Six present case examples of PE inaction; the projects span a range of contexts, are small- and large-scale, and are U.S.-based and international. In Chapter Four, Jean King reflects on her experience in conducting three mostly practical participatory evaluations (in the United States). One example is from a social service agency, another involves several participatory programs in an urban school, and the third explores a leadership-development program for school administrators.

Françoise Coupal and Marie Simoneau share in Chapter Five their experience conducting a transformative participatory evaluation in an international context. In this fairly complex process the authors, through the use of visual tools and local materials, trained twenty-eight participants (staff members of nongovernmental organizations and community representatives) to be PE facilitators. These facilitators, working in teams of three to five persons, then evaluated a set of projects that had been sponsored by the Canada-Haiti Humanitarian Alliance Fund. The authors describe this process, key outcomes, and, in ever-so-clear hindsight, lessons learned.

Chapter Six addresses the issue of scaling up PE. The authors present the results of a large-scale, federal, government-funded participatory evaluation in the United States led by John Gaventa. The Empowerment Zones/Enterprise Communities program, established by the Clinton administration in 1993, focused on revitalizing distressed urban and rural communities. Fundamental to this community-development initiative was a process whereby local residents themselves devised and monitored their own solutions to poverty. The evaluation centered around "citizen learning teams," members of which were trained to monitor implementation of the program and to track progress toward attaining key goals. Perhaps predictably, the local people were far more enthusiastic about the process than were the government officials, who were faced with conventional demands to obtain quick "results." The challenges of making PE viable in large-scale public-sector contexts were clearly reinforced in this evaluation.

A final commentary examines these case examples in relation to the theory. How well does PE work in practice? What are the practical challenges of working in a participatory way?

Elizabeth Whitmore
Editor

*ELIZABETH WHITMORE is associate professor at the School of Social Work at Carleton University in Ottawa, Canada. She discovered participatory research and evaluation while a graduate student at Cornell University and has since conducted a number of participatory evaluations. She has written numerous articles on this topic and continues to work actively in the field.*

*This chapter posits two principal streams of participatory evaluation, practical participatory evaluation and transformative participatory evaluation, and compares them on a set of dimensions relating to control, level, and range of participation. The authors then situate them among other forms of collaborative evaluations.*

# Framing Participatory Evaluation

*J. Bradley Cousins, Elizabeth Whitmore*

Forms and applications of collaborative research and inquiry are emerging at an astounding pace. For example, a bibliography of published works on participatory research in the health-promotion sector listed close to five hundred titles (Green and others, 1995), with some items dating back as early as the late 1940s. The vast majority, however, have surfaced since the mid-1970s. In the evaluation field, one label that is being used with increasing frequency as a descriptor of collaborative work is *participatory evaluation* (PE). The term, however, is used quite differently by different people. For some it implies a practical approach to broadening decision making and problem solving through systematic inquiry; for others, reallocating power in the production of knowledge and promoting social change are the root issues.

The purpose of this chapter is to explore the meanings of PE through the identification and explication of key conceptual dimensions. We are persuaded of the existence of two principal streams of participatory evaluation, streams that loosely correspond to pragmatic and emancipatory functions. After describing these streams, we present a framework for differentiating among forms of collaborative inquiry and apply it as a way to (1) compare the two streams of participatory evaluation and (2) situate them among other forms of collaborative evaluation and collaborative inquiry. We conclude with a set of questions confronted by those with an interest in participatory evaluation.

## Two Streams

Participatory evaluation implies that, when doing an evaluation, researchers, facilitators, or professional evaluators collaborate in some way with individuals, groups, or communities who have a decided stake in the program, development project, or other entity being evaluated. In the North American literature stakeholders are typically defined as those with a vested interest in the focus for evaluation (Mark and Shotland, 1985), although some authors prefer a finer distinction (Alkin, 1991). Stakeholders might be program sponsors, managers, developers, and implementors. Members of special-interest groups and program beneficiaries also have an identifiable stake in the program. In the evaluation literature arising in international- and community-development contexts, the term *stakeholder* is not explicitly used, nor is evaluation typically bounded by the parameters of a specific program. Nevertheless, consideration is given to the perspectives of various groups or communities within these development contexts, particularly as related to their involvement and participation. It can be assumed that many members of these groups have minimal experience with and training in evaluation or formal methods of applied systematic inquiry. Although the general principle of collaboration between evaluators and nonevaluators applies to virtually all forms of participatory evaluation, distinguishing features associated with goals and purposes and with historical and ideological roots help to delineate two identifiable approaches.

Garaway (1995) acknowledges that most applications of participatory evaluation combine rationales and attempt to integrate multiple purposes in a single evaluation project. Nonetheless, she differentiates between two specific rationales. Pursley (1996) makes similar arguments. Both authors subscribe to the view that one form of participatory evaluation is practical and supports program or organizational decision making and problem solving. We term this approach *practical participatory evaluation* (P-PE). A second rationale has as its foundation principles of emancipation and social justice; it seeks to empower members of community groups who are less powerful than or are otherwise oppressed by dominating groups. Our term for this approach is *transformative participatory evaluation* (T-PE).

**Practical Participatory Evaluation (P-PE).** Practical participatory evaluation has arisen primarily in the United States and Canada. It has as its central function the fostering of evaluation use, with the implicit assumption that evaluation is geared toward program, policy, or organizational decision making. The core premise of P-PE is that stakeholder participation in evaluation will enhance evaluation relevance, ownership, and thus utilization. The utilization construct has been traditionally conceptualized in terms of three types of effects or uses of evaluation findings: (1) instrumental, the provision of support for discrete decisions; (2) conceptual, as in an educative or learning function; and (3) symbolic, the persuasive or political use of evaluation to reaffirm decisions already made or to further a particular agenda (Leviton and Hughes, 1981; King, 1988; Weiss, 1972, 1979). Typically, impact is conceptualized in terms of effects on an undifferentiated group of "users" or "decision makers."

Shulha and Cousins (1996) describe several developments in the evaluation-utilization field that have emerged since the mid-1980s. First, many researchers have observed that utilization is often associated at least as much with the process of doing the evaluation as with the findings themselves (for example, Cousins, Donohue, and Bloom, 1996; Greene, 1988; Patton, 1997b; Preskill, 1994; Whitmore, 1991). Second, several researchers advocate an expanded role for utilization-oriented evaluators that incorporates elements of planned-change agentry (Mathison, 1994; Preskill, 1994; Owen and Lambert, 1995; Whitmore, 1988). Third, conceptions of utilization and evaluation impact are being extended beyond the particular program or target for evaluation to include organizational learning and change (Cousins and Earl, 1995; Jenlink, 1994; Owen and Lambert, 1995; Torres, Preskill, and Piontek, 1996). Each of these developments represents part of an integrated rationale for P-PE.

Building on principles of "sustained interactivity" between evaluators and program practitioners (Huberman and Cox, 1990) and on the observation that increased stakeholder involvement in evaluation renders the process responsive to user needs, several researchers have implemented and studied various forms of P-PE. Greene (1988) reported a study of an evaluation process that fairly closely resembled the conventional stakeholder-based approach (Bryk, 1983). Here evaluators assume responsibility for carrying out technical evaluation tasks, and stakeholders are involved predominantly in definition of the evaluation problem, scope-setting activities, and, later, interpreting data emerging from the study. Ayers (1987) described a similar model—the "stakeholder-collaborative approach," where stakeholders participate as partners, share joint responsibility for the study, and are primarily accountable for its results. A similar form of collaboration was detailed by King (1995). Cousins and Earl (1992, 1995) outlined an approach they labeled *participatory evaluation,* which built on the conventional stakeholder model by advocating joint ownership and control of technical evaluation decision making, a more penetrating role for stakeholders, and restriction of participation to stakeholders most closely connected with the program.

Despite the identification of countervailing influences, such as micropolitical processes or the lack of organizational or administrative support for the evaluation (Cousins and Earl, 1995; King, 1995), each of the foregoing researchers provide empirical evidence for the potent influence of these forms of P-PE in enhancing the utilization of both evaluation findings and process. Moreover, it has been demonstrated that under appropriate conditions participation by stakeholders can enhance utilization without compromising technical quality or credibility (Cousins, 1996; Greene, 1988). Process effects include influences on affective dimensions (for example, feelings of self-worth and empowerment), the development of an appreciation and acceptance of evaluation, and the development of skills associated with the act of systematic inquiry (Whitmore, 1988). Some of these process effects overlap with those emerging from T-PE processes described below.

**Transformative Participatory Evaluation (T-PE).** Transformative participatory evaluation invokes participatory principles and actions in order to democratize social change; it has quite different ideological and historical roots from P-PE. Most of the literature on T-PE relates primarily to participatory research and, later, to participatory action research, although PE is addressed directly at times. The background and principles are shared by PE. Based on a more radical ideology than P-PE, T-PE emerged in the early 1970s, primarily but not exclusively in the developing world—notably Latin America (Fals-Borda, 1980), India (Fernandes and Tandon, 1981; Tandon, 1981), and Africa (Kassam and Mustafa, 1982)—in part as a reaction to positivist models of inquiry that were seen as exploitive and detached from urgent social and economic problems. The work of these researchers was framed explicitly within contexts of power and transformation (Hall, 1992). An international participatory-research network was established in the 1970s, with headquarters in India, and the first of a series of major international seminars was held in Tanzania in 1979 (Kassam and Mustafa, 1982). These initiatives sparked a period of intense theoretical and practical activity in participatory research and evaluation. Although T-PE is now spreading to the university sector, it is deeply rooted in community and international development, adult education, and, more recently, the women's movement.

Dependency theorists saw conventional research methods as leading to cultural dependency and as denying the knowledge-creating abilities of ordinary people (Hall, 1977). The work of the Brazilian adult educator Paolo Freire has been pivotal in establishing the philosophical foundations of T-PE (1970, 1982). Other influences include some of the early work of Karl Marx and Friedrich Engels; Antonio Gramsci's notions of the "organic intellectual," hegemony, and civil society; Jürgen Habermas; T. W. Adorno; and the critical theorists (Hall, 1992; Maguire, 1987). Although the early roots of T-PE took hold outside North America, important work in this area has been done through the Highlander Research and Education Center in Tennessee (Gaventa, 1980, 1981, 1988), and the Toronto-based Participatory Research Group (Hall, 1977).

Several key concepts underpin T-PE. Most fundamental is the issue of who creates and controls the production of knowledge. One important aim of T-PE is to empower people through participation in the process of constructing and respecting their own knowledge (based on Freire's notion of "conscientization") and through their understanding of the connections among knowledge, power, and control (Fals-Borda and Anisur-Rahman, 1991; Tandon, 1981). No contradiction is seen between collective empowerment and deepening social knowledge (Hall, 1992); popular knowledge is assumed to be as valid and useful as scientific knowledge. A second key concept relates to process. How is the evaluation conducted? The distance between researcher and researched is broken down; all participants are contributors working collectively. Initiating and sustaining genuine dialogue among actors leads to a deep level of understanding and mutual respect (Gaventa, 1993; Whitmore, 1991, 1994). A third concept, critical reflection, requires participants to question, to doubt, and to consider a broad range of social factors, including their own biases and assumptions (Comstock and Fox, 1993).

Participatory research has been described as a three-pronged activity involving investigation, education, and action (Hall, 1981). Likewise, T-PE, by helping create conditions where participants can empower themselves, focuses not only on data collection, analysis, and dissemination but also on learning inherent in the process and on any actions that may result. T-PE has as its primary function the empowerment of individuals or groups. Rappaport defined empowerment as "both a psychological sense of personal control or influence and concern with actual social influence, political power and legal rights" (1987, p. 121, cited in Perry and Backus, 1995). In this approach, evaluation processes and products are used to transform power relations and to promote social action and change. Evaluation is conceived as a developmental process where, through the involvement of less powerful stakeholders in investigation, reflection, negotiation, decision making, and knowledge creations, individual participants and power dynamics in the sociocultural milieu are changed (Pursley, 1996).

Brunner and Guzman (1989) characterize T-PE as an emergent form of evaluation that takes the interests, preoccupations, aspirations, and priorities of the so-called target populations and their facilitators into account. "The social groups, together with their facilitators, decide when an evaluation should take place, what should be evaluated, how the evaluation should be carried out, and what should be done with the result" (pp. 10–11). In this sense, PE is an "educational process through which social groups produce action-oriented knowledge about their reality, clarify and articulate their norms and values, and reach consensus about further action" (p. 11). Initially, the evaluation team (comprising all participants in the project) may be fairly dependent on professional evaluators and facilitators for training, but they soon become more sophisticated. Ultimately, they are responsible for organizing and implementing the evaluation, disseminating its results, systematizing group interpretations, coordinating group decision making about project change, and ensuring that action is taken.

Much PE literature has emerged from the international- and community-development fields (Campos, 1990; Coupal, 1995; Feuerstein, 1988; Forss, 1989; Freedman, 1994; Jackson and Kassam, in press; Lackey, Peterson, and Pine, 1981; Rugh, 1994). As a result, a number of PE handbooks and assorted practical materials for grassroots groups have been published (African Development Foundation, n.d.; Ellis, Reid, and Barnsley, 1990; Feuerstein, 1986; United Nations Development Program, 1997).

**Comparison of Approaches.** Although these two streams of participatory evaluation are distinguishable from one another on the basis of their central goals, functions, and historical and ideological roots, there is clearly an overlap between the two. For example, it is difficult to imagine that participation in a P-PE project that led to an understanding of program functions and processes and to the development of skills in systematic inquiry would not, concomitantly, empower that program practitioner (or group). Equally, a T-PE project that led individuals to take control of their own development-project functions or circumstances would it probably also prove to be of considerable practical value in project development and implementation.

Apart from the overlap among central and secondary goals for PE, both streams overlap with yet a third rationale for collaborative inquiry. Identified by Levin (1993) as epistemological or philosophical in nature (or both), this argument posits that research knowledge and evaluation data are valid only when informed by practitioner perspectives. Although Guba and Lincoln (1989) argue this point vehemently, their approach to evaluation is not necessarily participatory, given the dominant role played by the evaluator in immersing herself or himself in the local context and constructing meaning from that perspective. Yet one can easily imagine that the development of valid local knowledge, based on shared understanding and the joint construction of meaning, would be integral to both forms of PE.

Thus, we conclude that P-PE and T-PE differ in their primary functions—practical problem solving versus empowerment—and ideological and historical roots but overlap in their secondary functions and in other areas. Despite differences that are evident at first blush, T-PE and P-PE have substantial similarities.

## Differentiating Process Dimensions of Collaborative Inquiry

We propose three distinguishing characteristics of PE. The first is *control of the evaluation process,* ranging from control of decisions being completely in the hands of the researcher to control being exerted entirely by practitioners. Control here relates particularly to technical decisions—those regarding evaluation processes and conduct—as opposed to decisions about whether and when to initiate evaluation. The second characteristic is *stakeholder selection* for participation, ranging from restriction to primary users to inclusion of all legitimate groups. The third characteristic is *depth of participation,* from consultation (with no decision-making control or responsibility) to deep participation (involvement in all aspects of an evaluation from design, data collection, analysis, and reporting to decisions about dissemination of results and use). A PE process can be located somewhere on these continua, depending on who controls the process and on who participates and how much. Shulha and Cousins (1995) observed that these distinguishing features correspond to basic dimensions or continua along which any given collaborative research project might be located. Cousins, Donohue, and Bloom (1996) made a similar case for differentiating among various forms of collaborative evaluation and between collaborative and noncollaborative evaluation.

If we accept that these three dimensions are useful for differentiating collaborative approaches to systematic inquiry, we might also consider that they may be independent of one another. Decisions about who participates, to what extent they participate, and who controls technical decision making can, in theory, be made independently of each other. Empirically such independence seems unlikely, but heuristically this distinction is a useful one. Figure 1.1 rep-

## Figure 1.1.  Dimensions of Form in Collaborative Inquiry

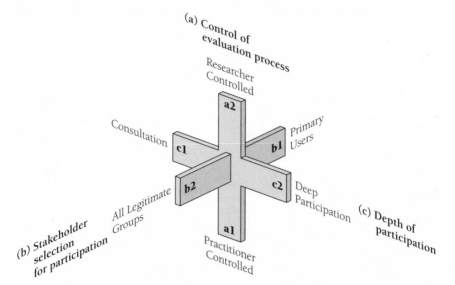

resents the characteristics in three-dimensional space. This device may be used to consider the collaborative processes associated with a variety of genres of collaborative and even noncollaborative inquiry. Any given example may be considered in terms of its location on each of the dimensions, thereby yielding its geometric coordinate location. We can now integrate this framework with our prior discussion of goals and functions in order to answer the following questions:

- How do P-PE and T-PE differ from one another?
- How do forms of PE differ from other forms of collaborative evaluation?
- How do forms of PE differ from other forms of collaborative inquiry?

As an aid to making such determinations, a wide variety of approaches to collaborative inquiry and evaluation are described in Table 1.1 and considered below. (Only representative forms of the various categories in Table 1.1 are discussed.)

   **How Do P-PE and T-PE Differ?**  Differences in the goals and functions and in the historical roots of these two streams of PE are explicated above and require no further elaboration here. After examining the dimensions of process, one might conclude that these approaches are quite similar, with the exception of who participates in the evaluation exercise. In the Cousins and Earl model (1992, 1995), the emphasis is on fostering program decision making and organizational problem solving, and evaluators tend to work in partnership with potential users who have the clout to do something with the evaluation findings or emergent recommendations. Although this approach

## Table 1.1. Forms of Systematic Inquiry by Goals and Process Dimensions

| Label | Principal Author(s) | Primary Technical Goal/Functions | Dimensions of Process in Collaborative Inquiry | | | Location in Figure 1.1 |
|---|---|---|---|---|---|---|
| | | | Control of Decision Making | Selection for Participation | Depth of Participation | |
| A. Participatory Evaluation | | | | | | |
| Practical Participatory Evaluation (P-PE) | Cousins and Earl (1992, 1995); Ayers (1987) | Practical: support for program decision making and problem solving; evaluation utilization | Balanced: evaluator and participants in partnership | Primary Users: program sponsors, managers, developers, implementors | Extensive participation in all phases of the evaluation | a1–a2 b1 c2 |
| Transformative Participatory Evaluation (T-PE) | Tandon and Fernandes (1982, 1984); Fals-Borda (1980); Gaventa (1993) | Political: empowerment, emancipation, social justice | Balanced: partnership but ultimate decision-making control by participants | All legitimate groups: especially program or project beneficiaries | Extensive: participation in all phases of the evaluation | a1 b2 c2 |
| B. Other Forms of Collaborative Evaluation | | | | | | |
| Stakeholder-Based Evaluation | Bryk (1983); Mark and Shotland (1985) | Practical: evaluation utilization; some emphasis on political aspects of evaluation | Evaluator: coordinator of activities and technical aspects of the evaluation | All legitimate groups: representation is key to offsetting ill effects of program micropolitics | Limited: stakeholders consulted at planning and interpretation phases | a2 b2 c1 |
| School-Based Evaluation | Nevo (1993, 1994); Alvik (1995) | Practical: support for program decision making and problem solving | Balanced: evaluator trains school-based personnel who do their own inquiry | Primary users: school-based personnel, mostly program implementors | Extensive: participation in all phases of the evaluation | a1–a2 b2 c2 |
| Democratic Evaluation | MacDonald (1976); McTaggart (1991b) | Political: legitimate use of evaluation in pluralistic society | Balanced: evaluator and participants work in partnership | All legitimate groups: representation among participants is pivotal | Moderate: stakeholders control interpretation and reporting | a1–a2 b2 c1–c2 |

C. Other Forms of Collaborative Inquiry

| | | | | | | |
|---|---|---|---|---|---|---|
| Developmental Evaluation | Patton (1994) | Practical: program improvement; evaluation utilization | Balanced: evaluator and participants work in partnership | Primary users: mostly program developers and implementors | Substantial: ongoing involvement and participation | a1–a2 b1 c2 |
| Empowerment Evaluation | Fetterman (1994, 1995) | Political: empowerment, illumination, self-determination | Participants: almost complete control, facilitated by evaluator | Primary users: usually key program personnel; sometimes wider groups included | Extensive: participation in all phases of the evaluation | a1 b1 c1 |
| Participatory Action Research | Whyte (1991); Argyris and Schön (1991) | Practical/philosophical: improve practice while simultaneously advancing scientific knowledge | Balanced: researcher and practitioner as coparticipants in research | Primary users: most often program implementors, although can be open to beneficiaries and others | Extensive: participation in all aspects of the research | a1–a2 b1 c2 |
| Emancipatory (Participatory) Action Research | Carr and Kemmis (1992); McTaggart (1991a) | Political: empowerment, emancipation, amelioration of social conditions | Practitioner: exclusive control; researcher as resource person | Unspecified: most often stakeholders who are disenfranchised or in some way marginalized by the system | Extensive: participation in all aspects of the research | a1 b2 c2 |
| Cooperative Inquiry | Heron (1981); Reason (1994); Reason and Heron (1986) | Philosophical: root propositional research knowledge about people in their experiental and practical knowledge | Practitioner: participants are both co-researchers and co-subjects with full reciprocity | Unspecified: most often participants are members of an inquiry group with all of the problems of inclusion, influence, and intimacy | Extensive: participation in all aspects of the research | a1 b2 c2 |

accommodates participation by others, potential users' ownership of and incli-nation to use evaluation data will be limited without the involvement of key personnel. Indeed, such unsatisfactory outcomes have been demonstrated empirically (Cousins, 1995; King, 1995; Lafleur, 1995). Part of the rationale for limiting participation to stakeholders closely associated with program sup-port and management is that the evaluation stands a better chance of meeting the program and organizational decision makers' time lines and need for infor-mation. Although the evaluator acts on behalf of the primary users by guard-ing against the intrusion of self-serving interests (mostly by holding program practitioner participants to the data and findings), the model is not as useful when there is a disagreement or lack of consensus among stakeholder groups about program goals or intentions. In such cases, conflict among competing interest groups needs to be resolved, and if stakeholder participation is limited to primary decision makers, the evaluation is likely to be seen as illegitimate and biased. For evaluators finding themselves in situations of this sort, the pru-dence of their acting in a conflict-resolution mode or their ability to resist being co-opted by powerful stakeholders (or both) raises questions.

However, T-PE more generally than P-PE involves participation by stake-holders, especially beneficiaries, members of the program, or the development project's target population. In this sense, power issues are more directly addressed. Of course, program beneficiaries are the population that T-PE is intended to serve through fostering empowerment and illuminating key social and program issues. Although evaluators and facilitators may have direct roles in training practitioners, dependence on such professionals diminishes as time passes and local experience is acquired. This may also be the case for P-PE. Cousins and Earl (1995) note that dealing with organizational constraints and integrating evaluation and participation into the culture of organizations are formidable tasks, destined to unfold over several repetitions and protracted periods of time.

Both forms of PE share the intention of involving stakeholders and com-munity members in all aspects of the evaluation project, including the highly technical ones. For practical and logistical reasons, Cousins and Earl (1995) question the value and viability of engaging practitioners in highly technical activities. In some contexts, however, community members may be better than evaluators at some technical tasks (Chambers, 1997; Gaventa, 1993). In either approach, the assumption that mastery of such technical tasks is a form of empowerment remains intact.

**How Do Forms of PE Differ from Other Forms of Collaborative Eval-uation?** In Panel B of Table 1.1, five examples of alternative forms of collab-orative evaluation are described. Perhaps the best known of these—stakeholder-based evaluation—bears the least resemblance to either form of PE. This may seem somewhat surprising, particularly in view of the fact that P-PE was conceived to be an extension of the stakeholder-based model (Cousins and Earl, 1992). Stakeholder-based evaluation has similar goals to P-PE but is perhaps better suited to situations where widespread agreement among stakeholder groups about program goals is lacking. By involving all legitimate groups in the process, the evaluator is able to pit those who subscribe to different value positions against one another while maintaining a generally neutral stance. In working toward consensus building, the evaluative process becomes more useful to a wider audience than would be the case if only one, or some, stakeholder groups were included. By controlling the technical decision making and by operating in the role of mediator or facilitator, the evaluator is better able to protect herself or himself from being co-opted. Whereas P-PE is best suited to formative evaluation problems (Ayers, 1987; Cousins and Earl, 1992, 1995), stakeholder evaluation is a viable approach to decision-oriented or decidedly summative evaluation questions. However, stakeholder-based evaluation differs from T-PE by virtue of its practical goals, evaluator control, and limited stakeholder participation in a wide range of evaluation activities. Although most authors describe its functions in pragmatic terms, Mark and Shotland (1985) suggest that emancipatory and representativeness rationales underlie the implementation of stakeholder-based evaluation. However, in a survey of evaluators, Cousins, Donohue, and Bloom (1996) observed that much of the collaborative evaluation practice in North America is aligned with the stakeholder-based model. Most of the reports examined suggest that practical decision making and problem solving were the forces driving the model's implementation.

Of the four alternatives to stakeholder-based evaluation listed in Table 1.1 (Panel B), two are more closely aligned with the more practical stream of PE, while the remaining two tend to resemble the more political stream. First, both democratic and empowerment evaluation are similar to T-PE. Democratic evaluation is intended to maximize the utility of evaluation in a pluralistic society (MacDonald, 1976). In this respect it is similar to stakeholder-based evaluation. Evaluators and participants work in partnership, sharing the work and the decisions. The evaluation is rendered democratic "by giving participants considerable control over the interpretation and release of information" (McTaggart, p. 10, 1991b). Stakeholders include all legitimate groups, a key point. To that end, representativeness among legitimate stakeholder groups and a cooperative working relationship between evaluators and stakeholders are pivotal.

Although similarly targeted on political goals, empowerment evaluation (Fetterman, 1994, 1995) holds as key objectives the empowerment of individuals and groups, the illumination of issues of concern to them, and the development of a basic sense of self-determination. Because these goals are manifestly emancipatory, empowerment evaluation is more closely linked to T-PE than to P-PE. But this approach, as described by Fetterman (1994; Fetterman, Kaftarian, and Wandersman, 1996), is in some respects enigmatic. In one instance, the evaluator acts exclusively in a facilitation mode, helping to support program or project personnel in their efforts to become self-sufficient. In another instance, the evaluator is "morally compelled" to assume an advocacy role for groups with less power and voice. Variation between these two examples of empowerment evaluation, both in the locus of control and in the meaning of participation, is considerable. The approach also differs from T-PE inasmuch as evaluators tend to work with those closely associated with the project being evaluated rather than with a wider array of stakeholders. Finally, Patton (1997a) conducted a careful analysis of the examples of empowerment evaluation compiled by Fetterman, Kaftarian, and Wandersman (1996) and concluded that many of these cases are exemplars of "participatory, collaborative, stakeholder-involving, and even utilization-focussed evaluations, and really do not meet the criteria for empowerment" (p. 149). This analysis suggests quite strongly that empowerment evaluation, in practice, tends to be best conceptualized as a form of P-PE.

Similarities with P-PE are apparent in descriptions of school-based evaluation and developmental evaluation. Nevo (1993, 1994) advocates developing "evaluation-mindedness" in schools through training, support, and school-based mechanisms for evaluation. Such mechanisms provide a basis for dialogue between school staff and those outside the school who request accountability, and although they are conducted internally and exclusively by school staff, they could feed into subsequent external, summative evaluations. School-based evaluation's focus on integrating evaluation into the organizational culture of schools and its focus on stakeholders closely linked to the program and their involvement in all phases of the evaluation are features that match those of P-PE. In developmental evaluation, however, evaluators work closely with program developers by helping them integrate evaluation into the development phase of programming (Patton, 1994, 1997b). In this model the evaluator works in partnership with developers, but stakeholder participation in the evaluation is comparatively limited. In a sense stakeholders represent the development function of the partnership, and although they are fully appraised of and able to shape the evaluation, their direct participation remains peripheral. This approach fairly closely resembles P-PE, with the exception of the depth of participation.

**How Do Forms of PE Differ from Other Forms of Collaborative Inquiry?** Although evaluation is directly linked to judgments about the merit and worth of a particular program, project, or innovation and thus provides a systematic basis to support decision making, forms of systematic inquiry designed for other purposes may also be carried out on a collaborative basis and are therefore worth comparing and contrasting with PE. Indeed, such comparisons have been made before (Huberman, 1995; King, 1995). In Table 1.1, Panel C, three alternative forms of participative inquiry are described. One of these, a North American adaptation of participatory action research (PAR), bears some resemblance to P-PE; another, emancipatory action research, is more closely related to T-PE.

As noted earlier, PAR first arose in the international- and community-development context but was adapted in North America in response to the limitations of other approaches in social science research. A distinguishing feature of PAR in North America is that it seeks to help organizations change rather than just accumulating facts and examining implications (Whyte, 1991). Grounded in three streams of intellectual reasoning—social-research methodology, participation in decision making, and sociotechnical systems thinking—this version of PAR is distinct from those forms of participatory research that entail collaborative social science research with no action imperative (Tripp, 1990). A variant is participatory action science (Argyris and Schön, 1991), which focuses on theories-in-use, including strategies for uncovering organizational defensive routines. In the general PAR approach, stakeholders who are members of the target organization participate both as subjects of research and as co-researchers. PAR "aims at creating an environment in which participants give and get valid information, make free and informed choices (including the choice to participate) and generate internal commitment to the results of their inquiry" (Argyris and Schön, 1991, p. 86). Inasmuch as the goal of PAR is to inform and improve practice within organizations, the approach links well with P-PE. There is generally a partnership arrangement between researchers and organization members, and the organization members take an active role in a wide range of research activities.

Emancipatory action research (also called participatory action research by McTaggart, 1991a) is more closely associated with T-PE but differs in important ways. This approach stems from the work of Habermas and is expressly liberative because practitioners come together with critical intent (Carr and Kemmis, 1992). Power resides in the whole group, not with the facilitator or with individuals or stakeholders. The practitioner group accepts responsibility for its own emancipation from irrationality, injustice, alienation, and failure. A variant stream is called critical action research (Tripp, 1990), which is fully in sync with the sentiment but stops short of action. McTaggart (1991a) does not find the distinction useful. Although many of these attributes are shared with T-PE, this form of action research precludes the involvement of conventional researchers, who are viewed, at least potentially, as members of the power elite.

Finally, cooperative inquiry (Heron, 1981; Reason and Heron, 1986), with its roots in humanistic psychology, is a form of research that arose in response to perceived deficiencies in orthodox approaches. In cooperative inquiry, "all those involved in the research are both co-researchers, whose thinking and decision making contribute to generating ideas, designing and managing the project, and drawing conclusions from the experience and *also* co-subjects, participating in the activity being researched" (emphasis in original, Reason, 1994, p. 326). Propositional knowledge about persons is derived both from their experiential knowledge and from practical knowledge concerns. Typically, the inquiry group is formed in response to the initiatives of certain parties or members, and therefore the group must struggle with internal issues of power, decision making, and practicality. To the extent that these issues are resolved internally, the group's work will be productive. In cooperative inquiry, trained researchers normally are not participants in the inquiry group. Participants engage in all phases of the inquiry process, including focusing, observing, reflecting, and deciding.

## Issues and Questions

We end by posing a set of questions for consideration. These are not necessarily new, nor are they unique to PE as an approach to collaborative inquiry.
Many of these issues are addressed in depth elsewhere in this volume.

**Power and Its Ramifications.** Who really controls the evaluation? How
does one account for and deal with variation in power and influence among
participants and between participants and the evaluator? How does one lis-
ten for the voices that have not yet been heard? How much should (or can)
an outside evaluator meddle in the affairs of others, especially when these
people need to live with the consequences long after the evaluator has left the
scene?

**Ethics.** Closely related to issues of power and authority are issues of ethical conduct and ownership of data. Who owns the evaluation findings? Who
has the power to dictate what data will be used and to what end? In what ways
can participants with less power influence these decisions? In some instances,
professional evaluators may witness the deliberate manipulation of data or
other mischievous behavior by participants. At what point do evaluators draw
the line and terminate their participation? Can or should evaluators just walk
away from such situations?

**Participant Selection.** Who participates on the inquiry team, and how
are participants identified and selected? The answers to these questions depend
on the nature of power relationships within the context. What are the implications for participant selection when PE projects arise out of external man-
dates from funding agencies or organizations responsible for initiating such
activities (or both)? What are the implications for participant selection in such
cases? How many participants? How will they participate and at what juncture? A related concern is practical. In projects involving participants from a
wide range of interest groups, to what extent is the feasibility of the project
compromised?

**Technical Quality.** How is technical quality defined? By whom? Are there
tensions related to data quality and the relevance of the evaluation to the local
setting? What criteria ought to be used in deciding what to do in such a case?
These questions are also related to issues of ownership and control.

**Cross-Cultural Issues.** How can cultural, language, or racial barriers be
addressed? To what extent does the technical knowledge and background of
the professional evaluator fit with the culture in question? Can the technical
knowledge be adapted or made to fit, and if so, how?

**Training.** How is the training of participants in evaluation and research
methods to be accomplished? Will training occur prior to the evaluation, during it, or by some combination of the two? To what extent do cultural and lin-
guistic differences intrude on training effectiveness? Can evaluators and other
professionals assume the role of trainer or facilitator with relative ease? What
sorts of training should evaluators receive as they develop professionally and
take on participatory projects? What knowledge and skills will be needed? Can

the knowledge and skills be taught and, indeed, learned in formal in-service and preservice training environments?

**Conditions Enabling PE.** Finally we ask, what conditions need to be in place for meaningful PE to flourish? What should participants' backgrounds and interests be? What constraints will they bring to the task (workload considerations, educational limitations, motivation)? Who initiates the evaluation and why? What are the time constraints? How will these issues be addressed?

These are the challenges we see for participatory evaluators and people interested in engaging in such activities. Credible answers to these questions will come only from sustained PE practice and particularly from practice that includes deliberate mechanisms for ongoing observation and reflection. It is our hope that both participatory evaluators and the participants with whom they work will report on their experiences, thus informing professional understanding of these important issues.

## References

African Development Foundation. *Participatory Evaluation Handbook: A Resource for Resident Evaluators.* Washington, D.C.: African Development Foundation, n.d.

Alkin, M. C. "Evaluation Theory Development: II." In M. W. McLaughlin and D. C. Phillips (eds.), *Evaluation and Education: At Quarter Century.* Chicago: University of Chicago Press, 1991.

Alvik, T. "School-Based Evaluation: A Close-Up." *Studies in Educational Evaluation,* 21, 311–343, 1995.

Argyris, C., and Schön, D. A. "Participatory Action Research and Action Science: A Commentary." In W. F. Whyte (ed.), *Participatory Action Research.* Thousand Oaks, Calif.: Sage, 1991.

Ayers, T. D. "Stakeholders as Partners in Evaluation: A Stakeholder-Collaborative Approach." *Evaluation and Program Planning,* 1987, *10,* 263–271.

Brunner, I., and Guzman, A. "Participatory Evaluation: A Tool to Assess Projects and Empower People." In R. F. Conner and M. Hendricks (eds.), *International Innovations in Evaluation Methodology.* New Directions for Evaluation, no. 42. San Francisco: Jossey-Bass, 1989.

Bryk, A. S. (ed.) "Stakeholder-Based Evaluation." New Directions for Program Evaluation, no. 17, San Francisco: Jossey-Bass, 1983.

Campos, J. D. "Towards Participatory Evaluation: An Inquiry into Post-Training Experiences of Guatemalan Community Development Workers." Unpublished doctoral dissertation, University of Massachusetts, 1990.

Carr, W., and Kemmis, S. *Becoming Critical: Education, Knowledge and Action Research.* London: Falmer, 1992.

Chambers, R. *Whose Reality Counts? Putting the Last First.* London: Intermediate Technology Publications, 1997.

Comstock, D. E., and Fox, R. "Participatory Research as Critical Theory: The North Bonneville, USA Experience." In P. Park, M. Brydon-Miller, B. Hall, and T. Jackson (eds.), *Voices of Change: Participatory Research in the United States and Canada.* Toronto: OISE Press, 1993.

Coupal, F. "Participatory Project Design: Its Implications for Evaluation. A Case Study from El Salvador." Paper presented at the joint meeting of the Canadian Evaluation Society and the American Evaluation Association, Vancouver, Nov. 1995.

Cousins, J. B. "Assessing Program Needs Using Participatory Evaluation: A Comparison of High and Marginal Success Cases." In J. B. Cousins and L. M. Earl (eds.), *Participatory Evaluation in Education: Studies in Evaluation Use and Organizational Learning.* London: Falmer, 1995.

Cousins, J. B. "Consequences of Researcher Involvement in Participatory Evaluation." *Studies in Educational Evaluation,* 1996, 22 (1), 3–27.

Cousins, J. B., Donohue, J. J., and Bloom, G. A. "Collaborative Evaluation in North America: Evaluators' Self-Reported Opinions, Practices and Consequences." *Evaluation Practice,* 1996, 17 (3), 207–226.

Cousins, J. B., and Earl, L. M. "The Case for Participatory Evaluation." *Educational Evaluation and Policy Analysis,* 1992, 14 (4), 397–418.

Cousins, J. B., and Earl, L. M. (eds.). *Participatory Evaluation in Education: Studies in Evaluation Use and Organizational Learning.* London: Falmer, 1995.

Ellis, D., Reid, G., and Barnsley, J. *Keeping on Track: An Evaluation Guide for Community Groups.* Vancouver: Women's Research Centre, 1990.

Fals-Borda, O. "Science and the Common People." Paper presented at the International Forum on Participatory Research, Ljubljana, Yugoslavia, 1980.

Fals-Borda, O., and Anisur-Rahman, M. *Action and Knowledge: Breaking the Monopoly with Participatory Action Research.* New York: Apex Press, 1991.

Fernandes, W., and Tandon, R. *Participatory Research and Evaluation: Experiments in Research as a Process of Liberation.* New Delhi: Indian Social Institute, 1981.

Fetterman, D. M. "Empowerment Evaluation." *Evaluation Practice,* 1994, 15 (1), 1–15.

Fetterman, D. M. "In Response." *Evaluation Practice,* 1995, 16 (2), 179–199.

Fetterman, D. M., Kaftarian, S. J., and Wandersman, A. *Empowerment Evaluation: Knowledge and Tools for Self Assessment and Accountability.* Thousand Oaks, Calif.: Sage, 1996.

Feuerstein, M.-T. *Partners in Evaluation: Evaluating Development and Community Programmes with Participants.* London: Macmillan, 1986.

Feuerstein, M.-T. "Finding the Methods to Fit the People: Training for Participatory Evaluation." *Community Development Journal,* 1988, 23, 16–25.

Forss, K. *Participatory Evaluation: Questions and Issues.* A report commissioned by the Central Evaluation Office, Occasional Paper 1. New York: United Nations Development Program, 1989.

Freedman, J. *Participatory Evaluations: Making Projects Work.* Technical Paper TP94/2. Calgary, Alberta: Division of International Development, International Centre, University of Calgary, 1994.

Freire, P. *Pedagogy of the Oppressed.* New York: Seabury Press. 1970.

Freire, P. "Creating Alternative Research Methods: Learning to Do It by Doing It." In B. Hall, A. Gillette, and R. Tandon (eds.), *Creating Knowledge: A Monopoly. Participatory Research in Development.* New Delhi: Society for Participatory Research in Asia, 1982.

Garaway, G. B. "Participatory Evaluation." *Studies in Educational Evaluation,* 1995, 21 (1), 85–102.

Gaventa, J. *Power and Powerlessness: Quiescence and Rebellion in an Appalachian Valley.* Chicago: University of Chicago Press, 1980.

Gaventa, J. "Land Ownership in Appalachia, USA: A Citizen's Research Project." In F. Dubell, T. Erasmie, and J. deVries (eds.), *Research for the People—Research by the People: Selected Papers from the International Forum on Participatory Research in Ljubljana, Yugoslavia.* Linkoping, Sweden: Linkoping University, 1981.

Gaventa, J. "Participatory Research in North America." *Convergence,* 1988, 24 (2–3), 19–28.

Gaventa, J. "The Powerful, the Powerless and the Experts: Knowledge Struggles in an Information Age." In P. Park, M. Brydon-Miller, B. Hall, and T. Jackson (eds.), *Voices of Change: Participatory Research in the United States and Canada.* Toronto: OISE Press, 1993.

Green, L. W., George, M. A., Daniel, M., Frankish, C. J., Herbert, C. J., Bowie, W. R., and O'Neill, M. *Study of Participatory Research in Health Promotion.* Vancouver: Royal Society of Canada, 1995.

Greene, J. G. "Stakeholder Participation and Utilization in Program Evaluation." *Evaluation Review,* 1988, *12* (2), 91–116.

Guba, E. G., and Lincoln, Y. S. *Fourth Generation Evaluation.* Thousand Oaks, Calif.: Sage, 1989.

Hall, B. L. *Creating Knowledge: Breaking the Monopoly.* Toronto: Participatory Research Group, International Council for Adult Education, 1977.

Hall, B. L. "Participatory Research, Popular Knowledge and Power: A Personal Reflection." *Convergence,* 1981, *14* (3), 6–19.

Hall, B. L. "From Margins to Center? The Development and Purpose of Participatory Research." *American Sociologist,* winter 1992, pp. 15–28.

Heron, J. "Validity in Co-operative Inquiry." In P. Reason (ed.), *Human Inquiry in Action.* London: Sage, 1981.

Huberman, M. "The Many Modes of Participatory Evaluation." In J. B. Cousins and L. M. Earl (eds.), *Participatory Evaluation in Education: Studies in Evaluation Use and Organizational Learning.* London: Falmer, 1995.

Huberman, M., and Cox, P. "Evaluation Utilization: Building Links Between Action and Reflection." *Studies in Educational Evaluation,* 1990, *16,* 157–179.

Jackson, E. T., and Kassam, Y. (eds.). *Better Knowledge, Better Results: Participatory Evaluation in Development Cooperation.*West Hartford: Kumarian Press, in press.

Jenlink, P.M. "Dialogue, Collective Inquiry and Organizational Learning: The Use of Focus-Group Methods for Learning." Paper presented at the annual meeting of the American Evaluation Association, Boston, Nov. 1994.

Kassam, Y., and Mustafa, K. *Participatory Research: An Emerging Alternative Methodology in Social Science Research.* Toronto: International Council for Adult Education, 1982.

King, J. A. "Research on Evaluation and Its Implications for Evaluation Research and Practice." *Studies in Educational Evaluation,* 1988, *14,* 285–299.

King, J. A. "Involving Practitioners in Evaluation Studies: How Viable Is Collaborative Evaluation in Schools?" In J. B. Cousins and L. M. Earl (eds.), *Participatory Evaluation in Education: Studies in Evaluation Use and Organizational Learning.* London: Falmer, 1995.

Lackey, A., Peterson, M., and Pine, J. "Participatory Evaluation: A Tool for Community Development Practitioners." *Journal of the Community Development Society,* 1981, *12* (1), 83–102.

Lafleur, C. "A Participatory Approach to District-Level Program Evaluation: The Dynamics of Internal Evaluation." In J. B. Cousins and L. M. Earl (eds.), *Participatory Evaluation in Education: Studies in Evaluation Use and Organizational Learning.* London: Falmer, 1995.

Levin, B. "Collaborative Research in and with Organizations." *Qualitative Studies in Education,* 1993, *6* (4), 331–340.

Leviton, L. C., and Hughes, E.F.X. "Research on the Utilization of Evaluations: A Review and Synthesis." *Evaluation Review,* 1981, *5* (4), 525–548.

MacDonald, B. "Evaluation and the Control of Education." In D. A. Tawney (ed.), *Curriculum Evaluation Today: Trends and Implications.* Schools Council Research Studies. London: Macmillan, 1976.

Maguire, P. *Doing Participatory Research: A Feminist Approach.* Amherst, Mass.: Center for International Education, University of Massachusetts, 1987.

Mark, M. M., and Shotland, R. L. "Stakeholder-Based Evaluation and Value Judgments: The Role of Perceived Power and Legitimacy in the Selection of Stakeholder Groups." *Evaluation Review,* 1985, *9,* 605–626.

Mathison, S. "Rethinking the Evaluator Role: Partnerships Between Organizations and Evaluators." *Evaluation and Program Planning,* 1994, *17* (3), 299–304.

McTaggart, R. "Principles for Participatory Action Research." *Adult Education Quarterly,* 1991a, *41* (3), 168–187.

McTaggart, R. "When Democratic Evaluation Doesn't Seem Democratic." *Evaluation Practice,* 1991b, *12* (1), 9–21.

Nevo, D. "The Evaluation Minded School: An Application of Perceptions from Program Evaluation." *Evaluation Practice,* 1993, *14* (1), 39–47.

Nevo, D. "Combining Internal and External Evaluation: A Case for School-Based Evaluation." *Studies in Educational Evaluation,* 1994, *20,* 87–98.

Owen, J. M., and Lambert, F. C. "Roles for Evaluation in Learning Organizations." *Evaluation,* 1995, *1* (2), 237–250.

Patton, M. Q. "Developmental Evaluation." *Evaluation Practice,* 1994, *15* (3), 311–319.

Patton, M. Q. "Toward Distinguishing Empowerment Evaluation and Placing It in a Larger
Context." *Evaluation Practice,* 1997a, *18* (2), 147–163.

Patton, M. Q. *Utilization-Focused Evaluation.* (3rd ed.) Thousand Oaks, Calif.: Sage, 1997b.

Perry, P.D., and Backus, C.A. "A Different Perspective on Empowerment Evaluation: Benefits and Risks to the Evaluation Process." *Evaluation Practice,* 1995, 16(1), 37–46.

Preskill, H. "Evaluation's Role in Enhancing Organizational Learning." *Evaluation and Program Planning,* 1994, *17* (3), 291–297.

Pursley, L. A. "Empowerment and Utilization Through Participatory Evaluation." Unpublished
doctoral dissertation, Department of Human Service Studies, Cornell University, 1996.

Rappaport, J. "Terms of Empowerment/Exemplars of Prevention: Toward a Theory of Community Psychology." *American Journal of Community Psychology,* 1987, *15,* 121–148.

Reason, P. "Three Approaches to Participative Inquiry." In N. K. Denzin and Y. S. Lincoln
(eds.), *Handbook of Qualitative Research.* Thousand Oaks, Calif.: Sage, 1994.

Reason, P., and Heron, J. "Research with People: The Paradigm of Co-operative Experiential Inquiry." *Person Centered Review,* 1986, *1,* 456–475.

Rugh, J. "Can Participatory Evaluation Meet the Needs of All Stakeholders? A Case Study
Evaluating the World Neighbours West Africa Program." Paper presented at the annual
meeting of the American Evaluation Association, Boston, Nov. 1994.

Shulha, L., and Cousins, J. B. "Utilization and Social Justice: Interconnections of Meta-
Evaluation Frameworks." Paper presented at the joint meeting of the Canadian Evaluation Society and the American Evaluation Association, Vancouver, Nov. 1995.

Shulha, L. M., and Cousins, J. B. "Recent Developments in Theory and Research on Evaluation Utilization." Paper presented at the annual meeting of the American Evaluation
Association, Atlanta, Ga., Nov. 1996.

Tandon, R. "Participatory Research in the Empowerment of People." *Convergence,* 1981, *14*
(3), 20–29.

Tandon, R., and Fernandes, W. *Participatory Evaluation: Theory and Practice.* New Delhi:
Indian Institute for Social Research, 1984.

Torres, R. T., Preskill, H. S., and Piontek, M. E. *Evaluation Strategies for Communicating and
Reporting: Enhancing Learning in Organizations.* Thousand Oaks: Sage, 1996.

Tripp, D. H. "Socially Critical Action Research." *Theory into Practice,* 1990, *29* (3), 158–166.

United Nations Development Program. *Who Are the Question Makers? A Participatory Evaluation Handbook.* New York: Office of Evaluation and Strategic Planning, United Nations
Development Program, 1997.

Weiss, C. H. "Utilization of Evaluation: Toward Comparative Study." In C. H. Weiss (ed.),
*Evaluating Action Programs: Readings in Social Action and Education.* Needham Heights,
Mass.: Allyn & Bacon, 1972.

Weiss, C. H. "The Many Meanings of Research Utilization." *Public Administration Review,*
1979, *39,* 426–431.

Whitmore, E. "Participatory Approaches to Evaluation: Side Effects and Empowerment."
Unpublished doctoral dissertation, Department of Human Service Studies, Cornell University, 1988.

Whitmore, E. "Evaluation and Empowerment: It's the Process That Counts." *Empowerment
and Family Support Networking Bulletin* (Cornell University Empowerment Project), 1991,
*2* (2), 1–7.

Whitmore, E. "To Tell the Truth: Working with Oppressed Groups in Participatory Approaches
to Inquiry." In P. Reason (ed.), *Participation in Human Inquiry.* London: Sage, 1994.

Whyte, W. F. (ed.). *Participatory Action Research.* Thousand Oaks, Calif.: Sage, 1991.

J. BRADLEY COUSINS is professor of educational administration on the Faculty of Education and director of professional development programs at the University of Ottawa, Canada. He has written widely on education issues, evaluation use, and participatory evaluation. He coedited, with Lorna Earl, Participatory Evaluation in Education: Studies in Evaluation Use and Organizational Learning.

ELIZABETH WHITMORE is associate professor at the School of Social Work at Carleton University in Ottawa, Canada. She discovered participatory research and evaluation while a graduate student at Cornell University and has since conducted a number of participatory evaluations. She has written numerous articles on this topic.

*This chapter traces the history and philosophical roots of participatory evaluation and examines some current debates in the field.*

# The History of Participatory Evaluation and Current Debates in the Field

*Sharon Brisolara*

Participatory evaluation (PE), a relatively recent addition to the program evaluator's list of resources, has been both held suspect and revered. As a model, PE combines ideas and practices that are still being debated in the field with those that have been formulated over so many years of contentiousness that they are now considered unremarkable. Many of these assumptions are well known to readers of this volume: the process of the evaluation (and what is learned throughout the process) is an important outcome of the project; stakeholders hold critical, sometimes elusive, knowledge about the dynamics of the program and the needs that the program is intended to fulfill; stakeholders can make valuable contributions at various stages of the evaluation process; dialogue among diverse voices is a means of approaching a holistic understanding of a program; the evaluator assumes nontraditional roles (facilitator, change agent, educator) in the interest of promoting collaboration; and the research process commits to actively applying what is learned in the service of people affected by the program.

J. Bradley Cousins and Elizabeth Whitmore (see Chapter One) have followed others in categorizing participatory models of evaluation as broadly reflecting either practical or transformative rationales. In the interest of consistency in this volume, this chapter will present the primary theoretical and practical antecedents of each strand of PE. Despite complaints to the contrary, PE draws from a rich history of exploration into the nature and role of social inquiry and of social inquirers. This chapter briefly reviews the philosophical antecedents, historical events, and evaluation models that have contributed to and interacted with the development of practical and transformative PE practice. These strands of PE need not be viewed as rival models of evaluation: both are participatory models that share a commitment to participation (some

NEW DIRECTIONS FOR EVALUATION, no. 80, Winter 1998 © Jossey-Bass Publishers would say to democratic pluralism) but differ in where they would align themselves on a continuum that ranges from practical (utilization-focused, within the status quo) to transformative (action-oriented, ideological). Given the considerable cross-fertilization between these two strands, the fact that PEs may be categorized as belonging to one strand or another, and the nonlinear evolution of evaluation models, attributing particular antecedents to one strand is rather artificial. With these caveats, the subsequent two sections of this chapter focus on the primary precursors of each PE strand.

## The Origins of Practical Participatory Evaluation

Practical participatory evaluation (P-PE) aims largely to support programmatic or organizational decision making by involving stakeholders (sometimes in a limited manner) in certain aspects of the evaluation process. P-PE differs from the transformative strand of PE in its emphasis on evaluation utilization and contributions to decision making, its conservative approach to action, and its reliance on the expert status of the professional evaluator. This approach to evaluation has contributed to a critique of orthodox social science practice, promotes inclusiveness (or democratic pluralism), and develops a praxis that blends utilization and action. Researchers and evaluators in the United States, Great Britain, Canada, Norway, and Sweden have been particularly active in the development of P-PE models for use in community projects, private organizations, and industrial settings (see Whyte, 1991). Much of this work appeared in the organizational-development literature and reflected a depoliticized collaboration between labor and management (Hall, 1992). Other typical settings for P-PE have been schools, collaborations between universities and community groups, and nonprofit organizations (Cousins and Earl, 1995). Organizations such as the Tavistock Institute in London and the International and the Latin American Councils for Adult Education have promoted the theory and practice of the participatory inquiry methods used within these settings (Hall, 1981).

Sociohistoric Antecedents. Projects such as these have developed in a context of powerful sociohistoric movements that have cultivated a re-visioning of participation, action, and research ends. In the United States, Canada, and Great Britain of the 1960s and 1970s, organized large-scale movements (such as the women's and civil rights movements) shaped a generation's consciousness of the role that gender, race, ethnicity, and class play in constructing knowledge and legitimizing "knowers." In the United States, the development of Community Action Agencies, the "war on poverty," and community and union organizing efforts led to the elaboration of action and consciousness-raising models. More recently, the challenges of a global economy have led many Western industrialized nations to reconsider top-down models of research and development in light of declining Western industrial bases. In the 1980s dwindling resources exacerbated by debt, recession, war, and a shift to a service economy led to increased competition for funds among businesses and nonprofits and a focus on accountability. Advances in communication technologies have abounded.

**Philosophical Antecedents.** P-PE's concern with participation is, in part, a response to questions posed by the critique of orthodox social science practice that emerged during the 1960s and 1970s. Important questions were raised. Is objectivity a critical regulative ideal? What is the purview of the inquirer? Who can be an inquirer? What can be known? How can aspects of social "reality" be known? P-PE has developed from a belief in the social nature of knowledge and knowledge construction promoted, in particular, by pragmatist philosophers such as Charles Peirce. For Peirce, a human being is an enmeshed "participant and experimenter in a community of inquiry" in which "human agency is the key for understanding all aspects of human life" (Bernstein, 1971, p. 177). John Dewey further elaborated many of these ideas. In his view, philosophy and education, and by extension social inquiry, were too distanced from life and human problems. He proposed emancipating inquiry by concentrating on the (ostensibly ameliorative) ends of research and focusing on understanding the interaction of the individual with her environment (Dewey, [1920] 1960, 1938).

Social science practice was to be presented with clear directions to these challenges by social psychologist Kurt Lewin. (Noffke, 1994, has also noted the action-oriented work of U.S. Commissioner of Indian Affairs John Collier in the 1930s.) Lewin's integrative work on education, action, social change, and culture motivated a group of social scientists to act on their critique of scientific practice (Brown and Tandon, 1983; Lewin, 1946). Inquiry based on Lewin's work places the "inquirer" in the role of the principal change agent who offers methodological expertise to the action-research process. Action is both means and end, should be appropriate to the social context, and promotes localized learning as well as theory and knowledge development. Changing views of curriculum and pedagogy in many countries and the action-oriented research attending these changes have both formed and been formed by action-research methods and models (McTaggart, 1991; Elliot, 1991). Within P-PE, action and utilization of learning are evolving, on-going, and central to the purpose of the project.

**Evaluation and P-PE.** Shifts in evaluation praxis have reflected and interacted with the theoretical developments mentioned above and, by extension, with the development of P-PE. Evaluators have not been exempt from acknowledging the methodological, epistemological, and ontological limitations of their work. Campbell and Stanley's work on quasi-experimental design and analysis (1963) was a significant catalyst for much of our post-positivist reflections. Weiss (1973) and Chelimsky (1987) remind us that our context and experience as evaluators, often highly political, constrain our actions and influence our practice in ways that we may not always consciously recognize. Indeed, evaluators now highlight the importance of situating program evaluations within their social contexts and responding to the needs manifested in those contexts. Thus we have seen explorations of program culture (Frost and others, 1991;

Preskill, 1991), as well as of sociocultural (Fetterman, 1993; Lincoln and Guba, 1985), moral-ethical (Schwandt, 1991), and political-economic (Chelimsky, 1987; Weiss, 1973) contexts. Increasingly, theorists and practitioners have voiced positions similar to those articulated by naturalistic inquiry, the idea that knower and known are inextricably related and that we are obliged to find new ways of demonstrating the warrant and credibility of our work.

A large body of work on utilization (Patton, 1997; Cousins and Leithwood, 1986; Weiss, 1972) has sparked fervent discussions of ways to cultivate utilization and action on utilization demands. During the 1970s and into the 1980s, the field grappled with questions such as, Who uses or needs evaluation? How can we promote utilization? Patton (1997) cites the importance of what he calls the "personal factor" in utilization-focused evaluation—that is, "the presence of an identifiable individual or group of people who personally care about the evaluation and the findings it generates" (p. 44). He further reminds us of the evidence in the literature that involving intended users (stakeholders) in evaluation processes leads to increased use (for example, Alkin and Law, 1980; Studer, 1978).

The integration of action, participation, and evaluation in P-PE is grounded in a commitment to democratic decision-making processes; P-PE largely assumes that democratic decision making is valued and has been experienced by stakeholders. Models such as Stake's responsive evaluation (1975), stakeholder-based evaluations (among others, Greene, 1988; Mark and Shotland, 1985; Stake, 1975), Wholey's approach to the development of program theory (1987), democratic evaluation (McTaggart, 1991; MacDonald, 1976), teacher research (Elliot, 1991), and Stufflebeam's decision-making approach (1973) have all contributed to P-PE's vision of democratic pluralism, stakeholder involvement, utilization through action, and the evaluator's role as facilitator or negotiator. Papineau and Kiely (1996) cite several of the above authors as promoting increased stakeholder participation with the intention of increasing utilization, representing multiple values and interests, and promoting the interests and input of disenfranchised groups. Others have suggested the benefits to be gained by grounding program theory in stakeholder views (Wholey, 1987; Trochim, 1985). Discussions about the wherefores and how-tos of stakeholder participation in the construction of knowledge and in decision making have increased: focus groups, Delphi and nominal group techniques, and structured conceptualization have all drawn considerable attention as methods for understanding multiple perspectives. Explicitly collaborative models, such as cooperative inquiry (Reason, 1988; Rowan and Reason, 1981), action research (among others, Stenhouse, 1975; Tikunoff, Ward, and Griffin, 1979), and action science (Argyris, Putnam, and McLain Smith, 1990), in addition to P-PE models, are benefactors of this work.

In sum, P-PE has responded to a critique of orthodox social science practice and a belief in the social nature of knowledge construction promulgated by pragmatist philosophers Peirce and Dewey, among others. Their work, and that of Lewin, further turned the scientific community's focus to the role of human agency in making sense through inquiry. Action is a concrete and direct manifestation of the utilization that many in the field of evaluation have worked so hard to promote. The field of evaluation has reflected on these ideas and has otherwise contributed to the development of P-PE. Among the most important contributions have been post-positivist admissions of fallibility, the attention given to holistically understanding (social and program) contexts, a focus on utilization of evaluation results, the benefits of involving stakeholders in the evaluation process, and ways of fostering and managing the participation of diverse stakeholders.

## The Origins of Transformative Participatory Evaluation

Transformative participatory evaluation focuses on empowering less powerful participants as a key process in fostering social change. It takes an openly ideological stance, one that seeks to democratize the production and use of scientific knowledge. The notion of objectivity is challenged by making explicit the political connections among knowledge, power, and control. Education and action, as well as investigation, are considered integral to the evaluation process.

**Sociohistoric Antecedents.** Transformative participatory evaluation (T-PE) has its experiential roots in the Latin America and Africa of the 1960s and 1970s. Many of the theorists and practitioners who contributed significantly to the development of T-PE are sociologists who found themselves faced with the dilemma of attending to or ignoring the human suffering that surrounded them (see Fals-Borda, 1987). Their work has most often been conducted in farmlands, squatter settlements, urban ghettos, and within the field of international development. Many Latin American and African countries were overwhelmed by war and poverty during these decades. Revolutions such as those in Cuba and Nicaragua, the advance of liberation theology in Latin American countries, and the movements and struggles that preceded independence from colonial powers for many African countries contributed to radical ideas and actions. "Favored" nations with high indices of poverty became recipients of foreign aid for "modernization" projects; others received arms and military aid that led to increased conflict. Participatory development, despite its frequent failings, became the prevalent model of development theory (Rahnema, 1990). Global economic trends (mobile assembly lines, decreased foreign aid, the rise of the informal economy) have contributed to cultural and social changes in many countries. Structural-adjustment loans and the subsequent requirements of the International Monetary Fund and other funding agencies have often exacerbated deteriorating economic and social conditions, particularly in the short term. T-PE practitioners have responded to such hardship by advocating engagement and radical social change, by analyzing and working to balance power in evaluation settings, and by clarifying the values that inevitably shape evaluations. Organized groups such as the Participatory Research Network, the Tanzanian Regional Workshop on Participatory Research, the Society for Participatory Research in

Asia, in addition to an international network of practitioners and the aforementioned organizations, have contributed significantly to the development of participatory inquiry (Hall, 1981, 1992).

T-PE, although influenced by the theory and practices that shape P-PE, draws heavily from revolutionary models of social change and of the power-in-action that permits, constricts, creates, and defines such change. Fals-Borda, who was originally engaged in what he called action research in the 1970s, notes the revolutionary work and writings of Gandhi, Che Guevara, and Paolo Freire, exemplars and developers of what he later called participatory action research (PAR) (see Fals-Borda and Anisur-Rahman, 1991). Saul Alinsky and numerous Latin American women's groups have also made powerful contributions to participatory organizing and consciousness raising.

**Philosophical Antecedents.** A clear ancestor to theories of radical social change was Karl Marx. Hall (1981) notes the field work of Friedrich Engels with the working class in Manchester and Marx's use of the structured interview with French factory workers as early manifestations of participatory research. Marxists and historical materialists have explored concepts such as alienation and human activity in addition to the modes, forces, and relations of production with the intent of realizing the ideal of human emancipation. Writing on method in political economy, Marx critiques the scientific perspective of his time: "The same men who establish their social relations in conformity with their material productivity, produce also principles, ideals, and categories in conformity with their social relations. . . . So long as they look for science and merely make systems, they [the proletariat] see in poverty nothing but poverty, without seeing in it the revolutionary, subversive side, which will overthrow the old society. From this moment, science, which is a product of the historical movement, . . . has ceased to be doctrinaire and has become revolutionary" (in McLellan, 1977, pp. 202, 212).

Marxists and T-PE inquirers alike are clear in their conviction that working to achieve emancipation requires more than a textured criticism of oppressive structures. Emancipation demands action and radical change firmly grounded in, but not obfuscated by, theory. Activity gives meaning to the theory, and the melding of both in praxis gives inquiry not only a political but a moral and ethical significance (Warry, 1992; Lather, 1991). T-PE challenges its adherents to respond wholeheartedly to the exigencies of praxis in the interest of meeting human needs. Inquirers within T-PE begin, continue, and end with the individuals whose lives are at the center of the evaluation. This interest is clearly set forth in Fals-Borda's description of PAR as an "experiential method, a process of personal and collective behavior occurring in a satisfying and productive cycle of life and labor" (1987, p. 330).

Among the most prolific and influential of those expanding on Marx's ideas have been Antonio Gramsci and the Frankfurt School of philosophers. These philosophers addressed the social, economic, and political problems of their day, exploring how analyses of inequitable systems (for example, social institutions) may be translated into organized action. Gramscian concepts, particularly the "organic intellectual" who leads from within an oppressed class (see Hall, 1981) and the "praxis of the present" (see Lather, 1991), have proved rich indeed. Interpretation theorists such as Charles Taylor, Paul Ricoeur, and Hans-Georg Gadamer sought to reveal hidden meaning through critiques of power dynamics and language as well as institutions (Rabinow and Sullivan, 1979). Both interpretation theorists and ethnographers have helped focus T-PE's attention on critically understanding culturally distinct forms of meaning production through engagement and by drawing connections between local and global dynamics (Thomas, 1993; Geertz, 1973). Action sociology, critical ethnography, dependency theory, and applied, social, and development anthropology are manifestations in these disciplines of the impact of these ideas. T-PE inquirers adopt a variety of roles in the interest of engaging the participation of people and their ideas; evaluators may act as change agents, empowerment resources, educators, co-inquirers, cultural brokers, or critics.

The possibility of emancipatory social change is predicated on an intimate understanding and willful manipulation of power relations. Power dynamics are not simply the direct manifestations of control, coercion, and influence. They are also pervasive and sometimes subtle influences on desires, opinions, and thoughts such that people perceive to be in their interest what is truly in the interest of those in power (Lukes, 1974). As Foucault (1980) has reminded us, everyone is continually and concurrently interacting within a ubiquitous system of power that prohibits and delegitimizes discourse as well as knowledge and also creates and reconstructs power relations. Individuals may be simultaneously privileged and oppressed, albeit in different areas of their lives (Weiler, 1991). Sites of resistance are also sites of struggle, and bringing internalized worldviews into the light of day enables people to occupy those points of resistance in the interest of increased freedom. T-PE, not surprisingly, concerns itself to no small degree with power dynamics. Practitioners have made analyses of sources of power, limitations on power, and strategies for sharing power central elements of their work.

Moving from power to empowerment was an important focus of critical theory as it emerged from the Frankfurt School; there have been many "critical" offspring, including critical social science, sociology, ethnography, and psychology. The aim of both critical social science as stated by Fay (1987) and the heart of PAR praxis as stated by Warry (1992) can be found in Marx's eleventh Thesis on Feuerbach (Bender, 1986): "Heretofore the philosophers have only interpreted the world, in various ways; the point, however, is to change it." For critical inquirers, the ethical starting point for research activity is equity in research relationships. The intention behind this equity is to work collectively toward understanding of one's self, one's place in the world, and the societal conditions that permit change. Empowerment and "enlightenment" are limited by our own enmeshment in tradition, sociocultural norms, physical limitations, and history (Fay, 1987). Nevertheless, communication and perception are imbued with many distortions and interests that are accessible to inspection and open reflection (see Habermas, 1971). In working toward empowerment, T-PE and its antecedents have drawn extensively from the work of Freire on strategies of adult education and his notion of "conscientization": an attempt to rise above oppressive and hidden discourses through organized action and reeducation that legitimizes "people's knowing" (Freire, 1965, 1990). Hall (1992) notes the concepts of horizontal communication (Gerace Larufa, 1973) and militant observation (D'arcy de Oliveira and D'arcy de Oliveira, 1975), and members of the Participatory Research Network as important pioneers of participatory forms of inquiry.

T-PE explicitly works to improve the human condition through social justice and equality. Feminist theorists have been instrumental in promoting the idea that a detached, uninvolved role for the researcher is morally unconscionable and professionally unwise given their privileged position and skills. An honest account of, and continued reflection on, ourselves and our values is necessary if we are to expose potential biases in our work, engage in reciprocal research relationships, and monitor our tendency to exert power or control over others (Reinharz, 1992). Feminist researchers and participatory inquirers have advocated for the use of our internal and external discourses, relationships, intuition, emotions, empathy, and experiences as sources of knowledge that represent human experience (Jaggar, 1989; Stanley and Wise, 1991). Participatory reflection on the dynamics and values inherent in the research process and context is a means of making sense of the world as it is, with all its contradictions, contingencies, tensions, and indeterminancies (Fonow and Cook, 1991; Maguire, 1987). Indeed, feminist theorists have suggested that participation enhances our confidence in our ability to know by ferreting out the underlying regularities that constitute our closest approximation to reality (Harding, 1991; Lather, 1991). Such regularities help us to understand what is and further aid in clarifying participants' notions (values) of how the world should be. Benhabib states that "intentions of the good life cannot be disassociated from the discursive practice of seeking understanding among equals in a process of communication free from domination" (1990, p. 122).

**Evaluation and T-PE.** These ideas and concerns are familiar ones within the field of evaluation. T-PE responds to evaluation's interest in the political nature of evaluation but further exhorts evaluators to engage themselves in action as "an inescapable responsibility" or moral imperative of their work (Weiss and Greene, 1992; Kidder and Fine, 1986; Whitmore, 1988). John Gaventa and the Highlander Education Center in Tennessee have been instrumental in promoting T-PE through projects and publications (Gaventa, 1980, 1993; Gaventa and Horton, 1989). Another important contributor has been participatory rural appraisal (PRA) (Chambers, 1994), an approach that emerged from a variety of sources including activist participatory research, agroeconomic analysis, applied anthropology, field research on farm systems, and rapid rural appraisal. PRA (now called Participatory Learning and Action [PLA] because it is used in urban as well as rural areas) was developed and promoted in the 1980s, particularly within agricultural-development projects. By the mid-1980s, the move was toward collaborative methods of soliciting information that was shared by and belonged to local participants. PRA emerged from such efforts, and today it is a model advocated by numerous development agencies including the World Bank, the U.S. Agency for International Development, and the Canadian Development Agency (Chambers, 1994, 1997).

We have seen the multiplication of participatory models. To those previously mentioned we may add morally engaged evaluation (Schwandt, 1991), emancipatory and critical action research (McTaggart, 1991; Noffke, 1994), participatory research (Hall, 1981; Jackson, 1980), collaborative action research (Fine and Vanderslice, 1992), and participatory evaluation (Weiss and Greene, 1992; Brunner and Guzman, 1989; Whitmore and Kerans, 1988). We can no longer deny the existence and pervasiveness of values (or, for that matter, theory as in Chen and Rossi, 1992) in our work; standards, interests, worth, and merit are all value-based concepts (Greene, 1997). The question becomes, Which values do we promote? T-PE mirrors the concern of normative models in stressing the importance of making ethical decisions and promoting critical thinking on social issues, particularly injustice and inequality. Others have urged the field to move epistemology beyond a realization of its inherently political nature toward regulative ideals that cede to the interests of the people who are the foci of our studies (Greene, 1997).

Finally, T-PE helps shape the field's critical reflection on multiplism. Recognizing the different perspectives (stories, paradigms, values) that collectively constitute the evaluation situation (Firestone, 1990; Howe and Eisenhart, 1990; Rossman and Wilson, 1985) and mixing methods in order to develop a holistic understanding of a program or problem (Kidder and Fine, 1987; Reichardt and Cook, 1979) are aspects of critical multiplism that have received considerable attention. Within a T-PE framework, multiplism serves as a source of legitimation, a means of including diverse, often silenced, voices in the evaluation setting, and a guide in choosing methods appropriate to the circumstances and suitable for training participants with diverse skills and abilities (Rugh, 1984).

Many T-PE practitioners advocate full, sometimes long-term engagement in projects in the interest of radical social change and social justice. Philosophically, these practitioners have drawn from Marx, Marxists, and critical theorists in developing theories of action and change. Power is an important construct within T-PE; feminist theorists, postmodern thinkers, and revolutionary individuals have been instrumental in clarifying how power is created, controlled, and reformulated. Feminist theorists in particular have emphasized the importance of articulating and making explicit the values that shape inquiry. The field of evaluation has struggled with many of these same questions, and the result is an interaction between T-PE and major themes for evaluation professionals.

## Current Issues and Debates in the Field

Critical questioning and reflexivity are integral to the PE process. Not surprisingly, PE models are also the subject of critical questions and reflection by both proponents and skeptics. Among the most pressing debates around PE practice are those that deal with the issues of objectivity, PE rationales (northern versus southern PE), technical quality, general usefulness, the appropriateness of empowerment as a goal, and the role of the evaluator. The central elements of these debates are the topic of this section.

**Objectivity and Bias.** One of the most frequent and apparently serious charges leveled against PE by its critics is that PE violates a long-held evaluation principle (or tradition) by forsaking an objective-as-possible stance for what some see as an inevitable slide into the pits of relativism. Immersion in a melee of divergent perspectives with little check on individual self-perception, critics argue, prevents evaluators from fulfilling their professional mission. Such work results in narratives from different perspectives: informative perhaps, interesting ideally, but not the stuff of evaluation.

Participatory evaluators disagree. Among P-PE proponents are those who suggest that we cannot remove ourselves from value conflicts: standards, interests, worth, and merit are all value-based concepts (Greene, 1997). Some advocate a value-honest, influence-neutral position for the evaluator that provides a full, textured understanding of the pluralistic values, beliefs, and knowledge systems of others through a dialogue and negotiation that ensures that no one voice has undue influence (Thompson, 1989). The evaluator-facilitator view is mitigated or bounded by strategies familiar to qualitative researchers, but honesty and openness allow the reader and stakeholders to detect where interpretations have been shaped by individual agendas or perceptions.

For many T-PE proponents, objectivity itself is a product of a colonizing science. Awareness of and reflection on values, opinions, personal histories, and power dynamics are viewed as more valuable foci of our activities. Some advocate going beyond the objectivity-subjectivity dichotomy altogether and moving toward a participatory mode of consciousness that reflects a recognition of the inherent inseparability of self and other (Heshusius, 1994). Lather (1986) suggests that researchers make their worldviews, values, and beliefs explicit from the beginning in order to provide a basis for later reflection on the extent to which their bias is reflected in the results. Marino (1997) asserts that there must be ongoing reflection on how (not if) personal bias is affecting the process.

**Northern Versus Southern Participatory Evaluation.** P-PE roughly corresponds to the type of PE used more frequently in the north—that is, the industrialized nations of the United States, Canada, the European Community, and Scandinavia. Northern PEs produced have often been more conservative with respect to action and change, evaluation elements, and the role of the evaluator. Southern PE corresponds to T-PE as it has been developed and practiced in the nations of the periphery in the context of development projects, agricultural programs, and communities. Southern PE models have often adopted more radical positions on methods, evaluator roles, and appropriate goals.

Apart from the obvious points of contention emerging from differences in praxis, debates have arisen around legitimacy and authorship. Northern participatory evaluators have often assumed or implied that methods of partici-patory inquiry originated in the north, beginning with Lewin and developing in a rather orderly fashion in Scandinavian factories and the halls of U.S. and British corporations and universities. Their writings ignore the southern liter-ature and experience entirely (Whyte, 1991). Proponents of southern PE vehe-mently object to this view, citing the early work of practitioners and theorists in Asia, Latin America, and Africa (see Hall, 1992). For southern evaluators and researchers, such undervaluing of their work, or blatant appropriation, is an example of the ideological hegemony and colonization that their efforts are designed to reshape.

Further, northern and southern evaluators often labor under different assumptions and circumstances. Northern evaluators are more likely to have greater material resources, including greater access to academic journals; these resources reflect a focus on legitimacy that privileges policymakers, scholars, and program funders and designers. Southern evaluators focus on the stake-holders, particularly the less powerful ones; dissemination is locally focused and often restricted by resources, the language requirements of many interna-tional journals and conferences, and the withholding of legitimacy by power-ful institutions. Debates concerning how to bring balance and equity among participants and how to engage in dialogue about both the issues that affect PE evaluators and the appropriate objectives of PE work are often truncated because the mode of sharing information is often internal to the PE model: northerners with northerners and southerners with southerners.

**Usefulness.** Even skeptics can acknowledge that PE is utilization friendly. Questions about its usefulness as an evaluation model often echo other spe-cific critiques. Critics have suggested that PE is more of an implementation strategy (regarding P-PE) or community development "dressed up" (regarding T-PE) than an evaluation approach. A specific criticism has been that PEs can-not be used to measure impact—that is, to answer the question, Does this intervention cause or contribute to the change(s) desired? PE efforts tangle with program interventions, muddying the evaluative waters in which one reads what has happened as a result of the program and what similar programs can expect.

PE proponents side with Chambers (1997) in an acknowledgment of the temporally and culturally situated nature of the dimensions of impact. With respect to impact, participatory evaluators ask different questions. What has been learned as a result of the program? Have we improved the quality of the program or services? Has authentic participation in the program increased? Cracknell (1996), writing on the experience of development agencies with evaluation, notes the emphasis in practice of attaining objectives through eval-uation. He notes development agencies that have promoted linking PE with impact evaluation in order to achieve results desired by both development agencies and PE: promoting sustainability, increasing feedback to "host coun-try" stakeholders and agencies, developing culturally significant and appro-priate methods, and negotiating the different values represented.

**Technical Quality.** Many evaluators who support finding alternative warrants for our work simultaneously advocate the importance of maintaining the technical quality of evaluation efforts. For P-PE proponents, quality is maintained through means similar to those adopted by their nonparticipatory colleagues—namely, evaluators remain responsible for ensuring the quality of methods and evaluation activities and their role as expert evaluators is central to their function. This attention to technical quality separates evaluation from other activities, maintains the integrity of the profession, and lends legitimacy to PE outside the local context.

Others, T-PE proponents among them, question the standard definitions of quality and argue that different measures are of equal or greater importance, such as ownership of the decision-making process, usefulness, change in the program and in social arrangements, and increased equity in the distribution of resources (Chambers, 1997; Hall, 1979; Pursley, 1996). Thus, technical quality as conventionally defined does not have a privileged status within their criteria. Different methods do not mean lower quality however. Chambers (1997) reports three case examples where participatory approaches were compared with conventional survey questionnaires. The participatory approaches proved "more valid, less costly, more timely and more useful" (p. 142).

**Power and Empowerment.** Although empowerment is frequently associated with PEs, not all those who use PE promote empowerment as a goal of the evaluative effort. Those who do not often view empowerment as a potential result of the involvement in the evaluation but not as a legitimate goal of the evaluation per se. Such a tangle of goals, they say, confuses evaluation with activities such as social work or community development. Participatory evaluators who view empowerment as a different enterprise may feel that evaluators appropriately advocate values other than empowerment such as democratic pluralism, dialogue among participants, or evaluation as a resource for program improvement.

Others, namely T-PE proponents, view empowerment as a critical element (and promise) of their work. Given that some people inevitably gain from an evaluation while others may lose and that evaluation is inherently a political process, one cannot escape this issue. The fundamental questions of who benefits from an evaluation and who loses must not be ignored.

Power and its implications are part and parcel of an evaluation, whoever participates. In a collaborative exercise, professional evaluators, by virtue of their status and expertise, are likely to see themselves (and are likely to be seen by others) as having power. In any group, some people wield more power than others, based on a variety of factors such as formal education, profession, class, race, and gender. More subtle attributes such as personality, interpersonal skills, and leadership qualities also differentiate people in important ways. The subtleness of these dynamics reinforces the importance of participants' being alert to them and building in ways to address them. Those who hold formal power may seek to suppress a report or reshape it in ways that meet their own needs, especially if findings are critical in ways that they see as threatening. The issue, then, is not whether power is an issue but rather how one uses it.

**Role of the Evaluator.** P-PE supporters often promote a traditional role for the evaluator as technical expert and often as the final judge of the efforts of the evaluation, sometimes of the worth or merit of the program. Moreover, the evaluator may have ultimate responsibility for technical quality but not exclusive rights to authorship or ultimate authority in the process (Greene, 1996). Other role demands are made within P-PE: an evaluator must be able to train participants, facilitate groups, and reconcile divergent perspectives.

T-PE professionals, however, are aware of the knowledge, skills, and abilities that they bring to the evaluation and work to promote recognition of the knowledge, skills, and abilities possessed by other participants. Their role includes ensuring that resources (and power) are shared and that different skills are valued. Engaged in the evaluation as a participant, the evaluator is involved in activities aimed at change or participation that may seem far afield from evaluation efforts as such.

These roles have clear implications for training of course. They go well beyond the technical expertise that has traditionally been the focus of our preparation. The use of PE implies that the theory and practice of participation in our programs and skills in facilitation, group dynamics, negotiation, and teaching in the evaluation context be part of our curriculum. Learning this set of skills is extremely demanding.

## Summary

P-PE and T-PE draw from rich philosophical traditions and from a wealth of experience in the field of evaluation. In explicitly addressing the issues of stakeholder involvement, evaluation utilization, active evaluator role, the objectivity-subjectivity continuum, critical multiplism, and the place of values within an evaluation, PE makes a powerful contribution to the development of evaluation practice and theory. The debates current among PE practitioners and the challenges posed by skeptics continue to form a practice that is gaining influence among those seeking solutions to today's social problems. It is, indeed, a much needed voice.

## References

Alkin, M., and Law, A. "A Conversation on Evaluation Utilization." *Educational Evaluation and Policy Analysis,* 2 (3), 73–79.

Argyris, C., Putnam, R. and McLain Smith, D. (eds.) *Action Science: Concepts, Methods, and Skills for Research and Intervention.* San Francisco: Jossey-Bass, 1990.

Bender, F.L. (ed.). *Karl Marx: Essential Writings.* (2nd ed.). Boulder: Westview Press, 1986, pp. 152–155.

Benhabib, S. "Epistemologies of Postmodernism: A Rejoinder to Jean Francois Lyotard." In L. J. Nicholson (ed.) *Feminism/Postmodernism,* New York: Routledge, 1990.

Bernstein, R.J. *Praxis and Action: Contemporary Philosophies of Human Activity.* Philadelphia: University of Pennsylvania Press, 1971.

Brown, L. D., and Tandon, R. "Ideology and Political Economy in Inquiry: Action Research and Participatory Research." *Journal of Applied Behavioral Science,* 1983, *18,* 227–294.

Brunner, I. and Guzman, A. "Participatory Evaluation: A Tool to Assess Projects and Empower People." In R. F. Connor and M. Hendricks (eds.), *International Innovations in Evaluation Methodology.* New Directions for Evaluation, no. 42. San Francisco: Jossey-Bass, 1989.

Campbell, D. T., and Stanley, J. C. *Experimental and Quasi-Experimental Designs for Research.* Skokie, Ill.: Rand McNally, 1963.

Chambers, R. "The Origins and Practice of Participatory Rural Appraisal." *World Development,* 1994, 22 (7), 953–969.

Chambers, R. *Whose Reality Counts? Putting the First Last.* London: Intermediate Technology Publications, 1997.

Chelimsky, E. "The Politics of Program Evaluation." In D. S. Cordray, H. S. Bloom, and R. J. Light (eds.), *Evaluation Practice in Review.* New Directions for Evaluation, no. 34. San Francisco: Jossey-Bass, 1987.

Chen, H., and Rossi, P. (eds.). *Using Theory to Improve Program and Policy Evaluations.* Westport, Conn.: Greenwood Press, 1992.

Cousins, J. B., and Earl, L. M. (eds.). *Participatory Evaluation in Education: Studies in Evaluation Use and Organizational Learning.* London: Falmer, 1995.

Cousins, J. B., and Leithwood, K. A. "Current Empirical Research on Evaluation Utilization." *Review of Educational Research,* 1986, 56 (3), 331–364.

Cracknell, B. "Evaluating Development Aid: Strengths and Weaknesses." *Evaluation,* 1996, 2 (1), 23–34.

D'arcy de Oliveira, R., and D'arcy de Oliveira, M. *The Militant Observer: A Sociological Alternative.* Geneva: Institut d'Action Culturelle, 1975.

Dewey, J. *Logic: The Theory of Inquiry.* New York: Henry Holt, 1938.

Dewey, J. *Reconstructions in Philosophy.* Boston: Beacon Press, 1960. (Originally published 1920.)

Elliot, J. *Action Research for Educational Change.* Bristol, Pa.: Open University Press, 1991.

Fals-Borda, O. "The Application of Participatory Action-Research in Latin America." *International Sociology,* 1987, 2 (4), 329–347.

Fals-Borda, O., and Rahman, M. *Action and Knowledge: Breaking the Monopoly with Participatory Action Research.* New York: Apex Press, 1991.

Fay, B. *Critical Social Science: Liberation and Its Limits.* Ithaca, N.Y.: Cornell University Press, 1987.

Fetterman, D. M. *Speaking the Language of Power: Communication, Collaboration, and Advocacy (Translating Ethnography into Action).* London: Falmer, 1993.

Fine, M., and Vanderslice, V. "Reflections on Qualitative Research." In E. Posavac (ed.) *Methodological Issues in Applied Social Psychology.* New York: Plenum, 1992.

Firestone, W. A. "Accommodation: Toward a Paradigm-Praxis Dialectic." In Y. Lincoln and E. Guba (eds.), *Paradigm Dialog.* Thousand Oaks, Calif.: Sage, 1990.

Fonow, M. M., and Cook, J. A. "Back to the Future: A Look at the Second Wave of Feminist Epistemology and Methodology." In M. M. Fonow and J. A. Cook (eds.), *Beyond Methodology: Feminist Scholarship as Lived Research.* Bloomington: Indiana University Press, 1991.

Foucault, M. *Power/Knowledge: Selected Interviews and Writings 1972–1977* (C. Gordon, ed.). New York: Pantheon Books, 1980.

Freire, P. *La Educación como práctica de la libertad.* Montevideo: Tierra Nueva, 1965.

Freire, P. *Pedagogy of the Oppressed.* New York: Continuum, 1990.

Frost, P., Moore, L. F., Rees, M. L., Lundby, C. C., and Martin, J. *Reframing Organizational Culture.* Thousand Oaks, Calif.: Sage, 1991.

Gaventa, J. *Power and Powerlessness: Quiescence and Rebellion in an Appalachian Valley.* Chicago: University of Chicago Press, 1980.

Gaventa, J. "The Powerful, the Powerless, and the Experts: Knowledge Struggles in an Information Age." In P. Park, M. Brydon-Miller, B. Hall, and T. Jackson (eds.), *Voices of Change: Participatory Research in the United States and Canada,* Toronto: Ontario Institute for Studies in Education (OISE) Press, 1993, pp. 21–40.

Gaventa, J. and Horton, B. "A Citizen's Research Project in Appalachia, USA." In *An Approach to Education Presented Through a Collection of Writings.* New Market, Tenn: Highlander Research and Education Center, 1989, pp. 220–229.

Geertz, C. *The Interpretation of Cultures.* New York: Basic Books, 1973.

Gerace Larufa, F. *Comunicación horizontal.* Lima: Libraria Studium, 1973.

Greene, J. G. "Stakeholder Participation and Utilization in Program Evaluation." *Evaluation Review,* 1988, *12* (2), 91–116.

Greene, J.C. "Qualitative Evaluation and Scientific Citizenship: Reflections and Refractions." *Evaluation.* London: Sage, 1996, pp. 277–289.

Greene, J. G. "Evaluation as Advocacy." *Evaluation Practice,* 1997, *18* (1), 25–35.

Habermas, J. *Knowledge and Human Interests* (J. Shapiro, trans.). Boston: Beacon Press, 1971.

Hall, B. "Knowledge as a Commodity and Participatory Research." *Prospects, 9* (4), 1979.

Hall, B. L. "Participatory Research, Popular Knowledge and Power: A Personal Reflection." *Convergence,* 1981, *14* (3), 6–19.

Hall, B. L. "From Margins to Center? The Development and Purpose of Participatory Research." *American Sociologist,* winter 1992, pp. 15–28.

Harding, S. *Whose Science? Whose Knowledge?* Ithaca, N.Y.: Cornell University Press, 1991.

Heshusius, L. "Freeing Ourselves from Objectivity: Managing Subjectivity or Turning Toward a Participatory Mode of Consciousness." *Educational Researcher,* 1994, *23* (3), 15–22.

Howe, K. R., and Eisenhart, M. "Standards for Qualitative (and Quantitative) Research: A Prolegomenon." *Educational Researcher,* 1990, *19* (4), 2–9.

Jackson, E. T. "Environmental Assessment in Big Trout Lake, Canada." Paper presented at the International Forum on Participatory Research, Ljubljana, Yugoslavia, 1980.

Jaggar, A. M. "Love and Knowledge: Emotion in Feminist Epistemology." In A. M. Jaggar and S. Bordo (eds.), *Gender, Body, Knowledge.* New Brunswick, N.J.: Rutgers University Press, 1989.

Kidder, L. H., and Fine, M. "Making Sense of Injustice: Social Explanations, Social Action, and the Role of the Social Scientist." In E. Seidman and J. Rappaport (eds.), *Redefining Social Problems.* New York: Plenum, 1986.

Kidder, L. H., and Fine, M. "Qualitative and Quantitative Methods: When Stories Converge." In M. M. Mark and R. L. Shotland (eds.), *Multiple Methods in Program Evaluation.* New Directions for Evaluation, no. 35. San Francisco: Jossey-Bass, 1987.

Lather, P. "Research as Praxis." *Harvard Educational Review,* Aug. 1986, *56* (3), 257–277.

Lather, P. *Getting Smart: Feminist Research and Pedagogy Within the Postmodern.* New York: Routledge, 1991.

Lewin, K. "Action Research and Minority Problems." *Journal of Social Issues,* 1946, *2,* 34–46.

Lincoln, Y., and Guba, E. *Naturalistic Inquiry.* Thousand Oaks, Calif.: Sage, 1985.

Lukes, S. *Power: A Radical View.* London: Macmillan, 1974.

MacDonald, B. "Evaluation and the Control of Education." In D. A. Tawney (ed.), *Curriculum Evaluation Today: Trends and Implications.* Schools Council Research Studies. London: Macmillan, 1976.

Maguire, P. *Doing Participatory Research: A Feminist Approach.* Amherst: Center for International Education, University of Massachusetts, 1987.

marino, d. *Wild Garden: Art, Education, and the Culture of Resistance.* Toronto: Between the Lines, 1997.

Mark, M. M., and Shotland, R. L. "Stakeholder-Based Evaluation and Value Judgments: The Role of Perceived Power and Legitimacy in the Selection of Stakeholder Groups." *Evaluation Review,* 1985, *9,* 605–626.

Marx, K. *Theses on Feuerbach.* (Originally published 1845.) McLellan, D. (ed.). *Karl Marx: Selected Writing.* Oxford: Oxford University Press, 1977.

McTaggart, R. *Action Research: A Short Modern History.* Geelong, Victoria, Australia: Deakin University Press, 1991.

Noffke, S. "Action Research: Towards the Next Generation." *Educational Action Research,* 1994, *2* (1), 9–21.

Papineau, D., and Kiely, M. C. "Participatory Evaluation in a Community Organization: Fostering Stakeholder Empowerment and Utilization." *Evaluation and Program Planning,* Feb. 1996, *19* (1), 79–94.

Patton, M. Q. *Utilization-Focused Evaluation.* (3rd ed.) Thousand Oaks, Calif.: Sage, 1997.

Preskill, H. "The Cultural Lens: Bringing Utilization into Focus." In C. L. Larson and H. Preskill (eds.), *Organizations in Transition: Opportunities and Challenges for Evaluation.* San Francisco: Jossey-Bass, 1991.

Pursley, L. A. "Empowerment and Utilization Through Participatory Evaluation." Unpublished doctoral dissertation, Department of Human Service Studies, Cornell University, 1996.

Rabinow, P., and Sullivan, W. M. *Interpretive Social Science: A Reader.* Berkeley: University of California Press, 1979.

Rahnema, M. "Participatory Action Research: The 'Last Temptation' of Saint Development." *Alternatives,* 1990, *15,* 199–226.

Reason, P. (ed.). *Human Inquiry into Action: Developments in New Paradigm Research.* London: Sage, 1988.

Reichardt, C. S., and Cook, T. D. "Beyond Qualitative Versus Quantitative Methods." In T. D. Cook and C. S. Reichardt (eds.), *Qualitative and Quantitative Methods in Evaluation Research.* Thousand Oaks, Calif.: Sage, 1979.

Reinharz, S. *Feminist Methods in Social Research.* New York: Oxford University Press, 1992.

Rossman, G. B., and Wilson, B. L. "Numbers and Words: Combining Quantitative and Qualitative Methods in a Single Large Scale Evaluation Study." *Evaluation Review,* 1985, *9,* 627–643.

Rowan, J., and Reason, P. "On Making Sense." In P. Reason and J. Rowan (eds.), *Human Inquiry: A Source Book of New Paradigm Research.* New York: Wiley, 1981.

Rugh, J. *Self-Evaluation: Ideas for Participatory Evaluation of Rural Community Development Projects.* Oklahoma City: World Neighbors, 1984.

Schwandt, T. A. "Evaluation as Moral Critique." In C. L. Larson and H. Preskill (eds.), *Organizations in Transition: Opportunities and Challenges for Evaluation.* New Directions in Evaluation, no. 49. San Francisco: Jossey-Bass, 1991.

Stake, R. E. "To Evaluate an Arts Program." In R. E. Stake (ed.), *Evaluating Arts Education: A Responsive Approach.* Columbus, Ohio: Merrill, 1975.

Stanley, L., and Wise, S. "Feminist Research, Feminist Consciousness, and Experiences of Sexism." In M. M. Fonow and J. A. Cook (eds.), *Beyond Methodology: Feminist Scholarship as Lived Research.* Bloomington: Indiana University Press, 1991.

Stenhouse, L. *An Introduction to Curriculum Research and Development.* London: Heinemann, 1975.

Studer, S. "A Validity Study of a Measure of 'Readiness to Accept Program Evaluation.'" Unpublished doctoral dissertation, University of Minnesota, 1978.

Stufflebeam, D. L. "An Introduction to the PDK Book." In B. Worthen and J. R. Sanders (eds.), *Educational Evaluation: Theory and Practice.* Worthington: Jones, 1973.

Thomas, J. *Doing Critical Ethnography.* Thousand Oaks, Calif.: Sage, 1993.

Thompson, R. J. "Evaluator as Power Broker: Issues in Maghreb." In R. F. Conner and M. Hendricks (eds.), *International Innovations in Evaluation Methodology.* New Directions for Evaluation, no. 42. San Francisco: Jossey-Bass, 1989.

Tikunoff, W. J., Ward, B. A., and Griffin, G. A. *Interactive Research and Development on Teaching: Final Report*. San Francisco: Far West Laboratory for Education Research and Development, 1979.

Trochim, W.M.K. "Pattern Matching, Construct Validity, and Conceptualization in Program Evaluation." *Evaluation and Program Planning*, 1985, *9*, 575–604.

Warry, W. "The Eleventh Thesis: Applied Anthropology as Practice." *Human Organization*, 1992, *51* (2), 155–163.

Weiler, K. "Freire and a Feminist Pedagogy of Difference." *Harvard Educational Review*, 1991, *61* (4), 449–474.

Weiss, C. H. "Utilization of Evaluation: Toward Comparative Study." In C. H. Weiss (ed.), *Evaluating Action Programs: Readings in Social Action and Education*. Boston: Allyn & Bacon, 1972.

Weiss, C. H. "Where Politics and Evaluation Research Meet." *Evaluation*, 1973, *1* (3), 37–45.

Weiss, H. B., and Greene, J. C. "An Empowerment Partnership for Family Support and Education Programs and Evaluation." *Family and Science Review*, 1992, *5*, 131–149.

Whitmore, E. "Evaluation and Empowerment: A Case Example." Paper presented at the meeting of the National Association of Evaluation, New Orleans, 1988.

Whitmore, E., and Kerans, P. "Participation, Empowerment and Welfare." *Canadian Review of Social Policy*, 1988, *22*, 51–60.

Whyte, W. F. *Participatory Action Research*. Thousand Oaks, Calif.: Sage, 1991.

*SHARON BRISOLARA is an independent program evaluator and evaluation consultant working in northern California. Her interests and experience include participatory evaluation, cross-cultural evaluation, the evaluation of development projects, and creating a culture of evaluation within organizations.*

*This chapter begins with a discussion of participatory evaluation as a set of principles and a process. Drawing on her own experience and that of other practitioners, the author highlights key moments in the implementation of this process, with an emphasis on the how-to.*

# Evaluating for a Change: Reflections on Participatory Methodology

*Beverley Burke*

*A white Canadian woman is asked to evaluate a women's program in newly liberated South Africa by its overseas funder, a Canadian nongovernmental organization (NGO). The NGO requests that the evaluation methodology be consistent with its main program goal, which is to empower the participating women. The report, however, will also be presented to the parastatal Canadian International Development Agency, which assisted the NGO in funding of the program. The proposed Canadian evaluator, whose primary experience is in social-change education, has previously coordinated participatory evaluations in the Third World as well as at the community level in Canada.*

This situation, in which I found myself not so long ago, suggests a few methodological issues this chapter will try to address. Who evaluates what and under what conditions? What decisions are made and by whom? What are the best methods to use in a given cultural and political context?

The purposes of the chapter are to share what I have learned from others and from my own experience about the principles and processes of PE methodology. The chapter is written from my position as an external evaluator asked to coordinate or facilitate a PE process. Although it also reflects my bias toward transformative participatory evaluation (as defined in Chapter One), many of the suggested methods and approaches are relevant for the practical participatory evaluator as well.

## Principles of Participatory Evaluation

There is no off-the-shelf formula, step-by-step method, or "correct" way to do PE. Rather, PE methodology is best described as a set of principles and a process of engagement in the evaluation endeavor. The principles discussed here have grown out of experience, of trying out different practices (Tandon, 1988; Sutherland, 1995; Chambers, 1997). Although all practitioners would not apply the same principles, and some principles are more appropriate to certain forms of PE than to others, the following set reflects the major points made in the literature.

*The evaluation must involve and be useful to the program's end users.* In a participatory evaluation, the group whose interests are directly and primarily influenced by the objectives of the evaluation must be involved (Tandon, 1988). I will refer to this group as *key stakeholders.* Who these key stakeholders are depends on the specific situation. For example, in a program evaluation of a grassroots NGO, the key stakeholders are the field workers and the community beneficiaries.

*The evaluation must be context-specific, rooted in the concerns, interests, and problems of the program's end users* (United Nations Development Program, 1997; Tandon, 1988). The evaluation connects the case (the individual project or program) to its larger economic, social, political, and cultural context (Hall, Etherington, and Jackson, 1979). Both the context and the purpose of the evaluation will influence the way the evaluation is planned and implemented. Appropriateness within a given context is fundamental to the effectiveness of the evaluation exercise and ensures that the results will be useful to program stakeholders.

*The evaluation methodology respects and uses the knowledge and experience of the key stakeholders.* Unlike conventional evaluation approaches, PE embraces the subjectivity of stakeholder perspectives. Expanding the notion of "legitimate knowledge," it values the experience and knowledge (however diverse and contradictory) that participants bring to an evaluation. The emphasis in this approach is on learning and knowledge generation for application and action (Pursley, 1996; Sutherland, 1995).

*The evaluation is not and cannot be disinterested.* Transformative participatory evaluation (T-PE) promotes empowerment of those having the least power in the context of the evaluation. These are often people who have been marginalized, with relatively little power or control over their situation in society. Practical participatory evaluation (P-PE) is interested in both evaluation use and in influencing organizational decision making (see Chapter One). In both cases, evaluation is most importantly and defensibly "interested" in the process and its results.

*The evaluation favors collective methods of knowledge generation.* PE is a collective process of reflection and planning rather than one where an individual presents conclusions based on his or her past work for others to use in future planning (Tandon, 1988). PE also recognizes that knowledge is deepened, enriched, and ultimately more useful when it is produced collectively (Sutherland, 1995).

*The evaluator (facilitator) shares power with the stakeholders.* The evaluator must be willing to "hand over the stick" (or pen or chalk) with confidence, recognizing the ability of people to exercise significant control over the evaluation process (Chambers, 1997).

*The participatory evaluator continuously and critically examines his or her own attitudes, ideas, and behavior.* This examination includes admitting and learning from mistakes, being critically aware of "what is seen and not seen, shown and not shown, said and not said, and how what is shared and learnt is shaped and selected" (Chambers, 1997, p. 157).

## Key Elements of the Process

To ensure that the principles of PE are embedded in the methodology, the following key elements must be included in the process.

*The process must be participatory, with the key stakeholders actively involved in decision making.* Not all key stakeholders will be involved in the same way or to the same extent. The field staff may form part of the evaluation team and help to collect data while community members participate in workshops to help analyze the data and develop the action plan. Participation must include stakeholder involvement in decision making. In the evaluation planning phase, specific ways of involving key stakeholders in all major evaluation decisions need to be identified. The key stakeholders take part in deciding when and how to evaluate, in selecting the methods to be used, in collecting and analyzing data, in preparing reports, and in deciding how the results will be put into practice (Feuerstein, 1986). The design of the overall evaluation must allow all stakeholders to see what the process involves and their own role in it, as well as how the pieces fit together. It should offer multiple and cumulative opportunities for participation. Most important, participants must be able to see tangible evidence of their contribution during the planning phase. The more that people perceive their influence over the evaluation process from the beginning, the greater will be their ability to gain control over decisions that affect their lives (Greene, 1986; Whitmore, 1988).

*The process must acknowledge and address inequities of power and voice among participating stakeholders.* During each stage of the process, special attention must be paid to balancing participation among the stakeholders. In the South African example, race was an important issue because the program was in a newly liberated country with a legacy of apartheid. At an organizational level, white women directed most women's groups participating in the evaluation. Gender was an issue of content for this evaluation, given the focus on women's programs. Gender also became an issue in participation when some women's organizations chose men to represent their programs. Gender also combined with other issues of social identity. Women with disabilities required the assistance of translators in workshops and favored methods that took their different abilities into account. Rural women's organizations required additional funds for transportation as well as additional efforts from the evaluation team members, who had to travel into rural areas.

*The process must be explicitly "political."* As indicated in Chapter One, T-PE is concerned with promoting social action for change and with transforming power relations in order to empower the marginalized (Lather, 1986; Pursley,

1996; Whitmore, 1988). P-PE recognizes the political nature of the evaluation process and advocates an expanded role for evaluators that includes elements of organizational learning and planned change.

*The process should use multiple and varied approaches to codify data* (Chambers, 1997; Hall, Etherington, and Jackson, 1979). PE practitioners often explore the same question from at least three perspectives on methods, locations, and groups in order to cross-check, compare, and gain insights. Varied approaches are also needed to ensure that methods of analyzing data are appropriate to local contexts and particular groups of people.

*The process should have an action component in order to be useful to the program's end users.* The action might involve assisting people to prepare future action based on evaluation findings. Once a concrete plan has been selected, the evaluation process should encourage participants to develop the broad outline and to fill in the details following the evaluation exercise. In a T-PE process, short-term actions need to contribute to the long-term goal of improving social and economic conditions.

*The process should explicitly aim to build capacity, especially evaluation capacity, so that stakeholders can control future evaluation processes.* In some evaluations capacity building starts early, in the planning phase. There is usually an introduction to PE, designed to help all participants understand the process and their roles and how PE differs from other evaluation processes they might have experienced. Participants are more likely to become engaged in the process when they fully understand the suggested approach. In many cases group members are also trained to collect data. Workshops are held on how to facilitate a focus group, conduct an interview, or use various tools for collecting quantitative data. Many participatory methods used in the evaluation process can be applied by participants to other aspects of their work—in education and action research, for example. In the longer term, such skills will help to strengthen both the individuals and the program and to reduce dependence on outside experts or evaluators (Hall, Etherington, and Jackson, 1979).

*The process must be educational.* PE involves individual and collective learning. Evaluation participants learn from one another about their individual and collective strengths and weaknesses, about ways to improve their programs, and about understanding and intervening in their social reality. Not only the outcomes of the evaluation but the involvement in the process itself provide insights and learning (Tandon, 1988).

## Implementing the Process

This is all very well, you might say. We understand the underlying principles and the key elements in the process, but how do we do it? Although there is no formula to follow when undertaking a PE, at some key moments in the process important decisions are made. This process builds on the spiral-design model, developed as a methodology for social-change education (Arnold and others, 1991), which is similar to the dialectical methodology (action-reflection-action) of popular education (Freire, 1970). In this section I suggest some questions and methods for the practitioner to ask and apply at each key moment identified in Figure 3.1.

**Deciding to Do It.** Two questions need to be answered at the beginning of the process. First, who decides? When the key stakeholders themselves request the evaluation, they need to be encouraged to think about what it is they want to learn. An outside evaluator can help identify important questions and suggest resources, like the how-to manuals referenced at the end of this chapter (Arnold and others, 1991; Ellis, Reid and Barnsley, 1990; Feuerstein, 1986; United Nations Development Program, 1997; marino, 1997). When the donor agency (which controls the funding) requests the evaluation, the evaluator should try to confirm that key stakeholders are in agreement with this decision. The evaluator may also encourage the group concerned to negotiate the terms and process of the evaluation with the funders (Ellis, Reid, and Barnsley, 1990).

Second, under what conditions? Those involved as outside evaluators need to ensure that certain conditions are met in order for the PE process to be successful. These are some of the conditions that I attempt to negotiate before agreeing to conduct a PE (United Nations Development Program, 1997):

• The program or project has a clearly identified group of key stakeholders who support the evaluation, even if it is initiated by the funder.

**Figure 3.1. Key Moments and Decisions in the Evaluation Process**

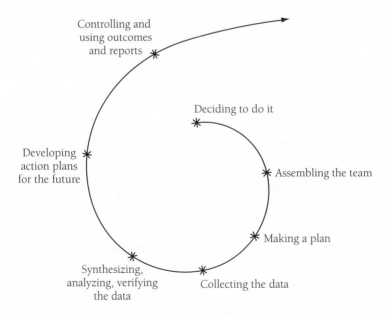

- There is evidence that key stakeholders have thought about what they would like to learn from the evaluation.
- All stakeholders, especially funders and those holding the most power within the organization(s) under review, have an understanding of and are in agreement with the PE process.
- There is an internal evaluation team with sufficient time and interest to assist outside evaluators in planning and implementing the evaluation.
- Resources (both time and money) are sufficient to ensure meaningful participation and capacity building. If an organization is not willing to allocate either time or money, the PE approach is not a desirable option.

An initial draft stating the terms of reference is usually prepared by the funding organization to facilitate the hiring of external evaluators. However, detailed terms of reference are developed in a workshop with key stakeholders (as outlined below).

Because control over the budget for an evaluation constitutes power, money is an issue that needs to be on the table from the start. Some community groups have been able to negotiate with donor agencies to have joint signatures (donor and key stakeholder representatives) on contracts and to have checks issued during the evaluation process. Where this is not possible, the existence of a power imbalance needs to be at least acknowledged, and the budget process and information need to be shared with key stakeholders.

The costs of using a participatory process should be understood. One major issue is the increased burden placed on both evaluators and stakeholders by this approach. It takes a great deal of time to ensure that participants are involved in all the major evaluation decisions, to build understanding of the process and what is involved, to train those who are to be involved, and to develop instruments and methods adapted to the context. Meaningful participation by key stakeholders requires that time be set aside from other work; some practitioners caution against overburdening the key stakeholders (Ellis, Reid, and Barnsley, 1990; Greene, 1986). As a result of the extra time required, PEs can sometimes be more expensive than other approaches.

However, there is a cost to not using PE. With low involvement by the key stakeholders, there is a risk that program beneficiaries will lose a sense of ownership of the evaluation findings. PE needs to be seen as an investment in the future. Stakeholder involvement in the evaluation process leads to increased utilization of evaluation results (Greene, 1986; Preskill and Caracelli, 1996). And, as noted earlier, PEs provide added value in capacity-building activities and program-development components that other approaches do not deliver.

**Assembling the Team.** As has been discussed earlier, PE attempts to change the relations between evaluators and key stakeholders, with an emphasis on power sharing. In addition to the role of traditional methodological and technical expert, a participatory evaluator's roles may include that of educator, learner, facilitator, coordinator, arbitrator, or even negotiator (Feuerstein, 1986; Tandon, 1988).

A number of issues need to be considered when choosing a PE team. For these decisions I have found Greene (1986), Feuerstein (1986), and Tandon (1988) especially helpful.

*Internal or External Evaluators?* An important decision in a PE process is whether to use internal or external evaluators. The advantages and disadvantages of each option are well known to most evaluators and are not necessarily unique to PE.

Tandon (1988) suggests that some organizations have the capacity to undertake their own evaluations without assistance from outsiders. When outsiders are asked to facilitate the process, he suggests that their role should be to help raise issues and questions that may be overlooked or difficult to raise, to help create methods of data collection and analysis, and to help organization members take charge of the process and use it in their own interest. The external person must ensure that the organization "owns" the evaluation process.

My experience suggests that an internal-external team can work well. Tasks can be shared by an internal team and outside evaluators. An internal team can be a small working group representing the key stakeholders, formed with attention to geography, race, gender, and other issues of social identity that will have an impact on the evaluation. Considerations of location and social identity also apply to the choice of the external evaluator(s). For example, in a Latin American evaluation, a Canadian could be paired with a local evaluator.

The working group of key stakeholders is chiefly responsible for identifying and directing the substantive or programmatic content of the evaluation, while the outside evaluators facilitate the process and are responsible for structuring the evaluation as well as the technical work. Each can and does participate in the other's areas. For example, key stakeholders are often intimately involved in developing the evaluation plan and may be involved in data collection. The outside evaluators have input into evaluation questions and content. Both teams develop conclusions and recommendations.

Issues related to bias, often raised in connection with the role of the evaluator, have been discussed in Chapter Two so will not be repeated here.

*Skills and Abilities of Evaluators.* As described by Garaway (1995), Feuerstein (1986), Tandon (1988), Sutherland (1995), and United Nations Development Program (1997), these are some of the key characteristics required of participatory evaluators:

- Personal commitment to an interactive process and the principles of PE.
- Ability to work as part of a team.
- Technical expertise and training in a wide variety of research techniques and methodologies, with emphasis on participatory methodologies.

- Group facilitation skills, including understanding group process, dealing with tensions and conflict, equalizing participation, running participatory activities, summarizing, and being an active listener.
- Ability to communicate with different kinds of stakeholders, such as members of grassroots groups, government representatives, and representatives of international donor agencies.
- Teaching skills, the ability to communicate evaluation methodology, and adaptability to a variety of teaching contexts.

The skills required for effective group facilitation pose particular challenges for traditionally trained evaluators. Greene (1986) notes.a major lesson that emerged in the PE case studies she conducted: that her own technical skills and teaching experience provided good support for all roles except that of facilitator. She states that it is unreasonable to expect a single evaluator to have all the requisite skills, and she suggests a team approach.

**Making a Plan.** Devising a concrete plan for the evaluation has two phases: orienting key stakeholders to PE and setting the agenda.

*Orientation to Participatory Evaluation.* For the key stakeholders to play an active role in designing the evaluation, they need to understand what it is all about. Therefore, the external evaluator should provide background on the PE approach as it applies to the context of the evaluation. In my experience, the best format for supplying this information is a workshop. In small organizations, as many members as possible should attend. In large evaluations, those involving a number of organizations and locations, several sessions may have to be held. (For a sample agenda, see Sutherland, 1995.) During the workshop detailed "terms of reference" need to be developed. They determine who will do what, and they also make the decision-making process transparent, deal with issues of confidentiality and control of data, and affirm the importance of group ownership of the process. Some evaluators have found it helpful to develop a contract for working together as part of setting the terms of reference, not just for the evaluation team but for all participants (Sutherland, 1995).

When several workshops are to be held, it is important that the internal members represent participants across all workshops. It is also helpful to share workshop results across groups and to identify for further discussion any fundamental disagreements.

When it is not possible to have a workshop with all key stakeholders, other methods may be used. In the South African example, materials on PE were sent to the participating organizations as background for their initial internal discussions. A questionnaire followed asking people what they wanted to get out of the evaluation and suggesting a process for collectively filling out the questionnaire. This method was not entirely satisfactory in this case, however, because it assumed literacy and a command of English.

*Setting the Agenda.* Although the initial workshop(s) will provide invaluable input as to what people want to learn from the evaluation, the evaluation team will still need to finalize their goals and objectives and continue to clarify the main question: who wants to know what and why?

Sometimes a series of shorter meetings with key stakeholders may be required to discuss indicators for each goal, who should be asked for what information, and what methods will be used to collect the information for each constituency. The more people involved in this process, the greater chance it has to meet its goals of empowerment and utilization. In small organizations it is feasible to include a number of representatives from different levels of the organization in one session—staff, community participants, field workers, board members. In large programs, those involving several organizations or countries or regions, the process will be longer. For example, in a multicountry evaluation in the Caribbean, we trained local evaluators, chosen by participating groups in each country, to facilitate local workshops and gather input on the evaluation plan. We then put the plan together in consultation with local evaluators.

As has been suggested by Sutherland (1995), the planning workshop is also useful for constructing a historical overview of the work to be evaluated and for situating it within the broad organizational, social, political, cultural, and economic context. By adapting the historical time-line method (Barndt, 1989), participants can develop a chronological depiction on newsprint posted on a wall, illustrating the major developments in the program and noting (above the line) external influences that affect their work and (below the line) internal organizational influences. This time line can then be used as a resource in the data-collection phase of the evaluation.

**Collecting the Data.** Participatory evaluators need to decide who will be involved in collecting data and what methods will be used.

*Deciding Who Will Collect Data.* Collecting data is another way to involve key stakeholders, with adequate methodological training provided by the external evaluation team. In small organizations training can be provided to all members interested in learning these skills, whether or not they will be directly involved as data collectors. Triangulation, where evaluation team members meet regularly to cross-check and verify the process and the data, is a simple research tool that can be used throughout the evaluation (United Nations Development Program, 1997).

In the Caribbean example mentioned above, local evaluators, who had been chosen by the participating groups, conducted the interviews and workshops. As evaluation coordinators we provided training for the local evaluators and, with their help, developed the tools and methods to be used. Following the evaluation, the local evaluators were able to provide training workshops for their respective groups.

*Choosing and Adapting Methods.* As Garaway (1995) points out, in many ways the data-collection methods used in PE are not very different from the multimethod approaches that have gained currency in the evaluation field as a whole. They share guidelines for considering the evaluation questions and the kind of data required. In PE, however, questions of whose interests are served and who is listened to influence the choice of methods (Pursley, 1996). The following are some additional considerations for adapting standard methods for PEs:

- *Technical difficulty and adaptability to a particular level of expertise.* The methods chosen should build confidence, not be overpowering. If local people are trained in the use of methods, their level of experience and expertise needs to be taken into account. Methods should also lend themselves to future use by local organizations for their own evaluation processes. Locally accessible technology and materials as well as space and logistics will also have a bearing on the choice of methods. For example, instead of using complex equipment and pH levels to measure soil acidity, one might rely on simple tasting or smelling of the soil by an experienced local farmer (Stuart, 1994).

- *Cultural appropriateness.* We need to take into account ways people feel comfortable learning, communicating, and interacting, which are influenced by many variables including race, class, gender, and geographical location. Although cultural appropriateness should be a criterion for all evaluation methods, it is of particular importance for T-PEs, given their goal of empowering those most affected by the program being reviewed. Determining cultural appropriateness can be very complicated. For example, an evaluation of a development program in South Africa, where the donor agency was Canadian, put decision making in the hands of white men. The implementation staff members were all women. Many of those in charge of the local organizations were urban white women or urban white and black men, although most of the beneficiaries were rural black women. Such discrepancies are not confined to Third World evaluations. A middle-class person conducting an evaluation in a working-class organization or an academic working with a community group in Toronto will also face issues of cultural appropriateness.

- *Facilitation of learning.* The methods used should facilitate learning. They should help people take control and feel empowered and should lead them to value and express their own knowledge and viewpoints.

- *Barriers to participation.* The choice of methods needs to take into account obstacles to stakeholder participation. For example, the level of literacy, command of the main language used in the evaluation, social class, gender, race, physical challenge, age, geography, and time constraints are all potential barriers.

In addition, traditional methods may need to be adapted. For example, participant observation is a helpful method in a PE, but the observation is not hidden from participants and not necessarily a task assigned to the external evaluator. Charts, tests, and other measuring devices are often generated locally to ensure they are easy to use and applicable in the local context (Chambers, 1997). Interviews are conducted in an interactive, dialogical way, with the interviewer often sharing information on his or her background as well as asking questions. Sequential interviews are used with individual interviews followed by group sessions.

The following are methods particularly suited to a participatory approach (Arnold and others, 1991; Garaway, 1995; Sutherland, 1995).

- Pictures drawn by individuals and groups
- Group mapping and modeling
- Problem stories using real events that are evaluated by the group
- Creative expression—drama, role plays, songs, dances, sculpturing (a collective presentation in which people use themselves to present a situation or theme in silence, without movement)
- Diaries
- Case studies
- Group meetings, workshops, focus groups
- Murals and time lines
- Web charts (to trace the root causes or implications of a specific phenomenon)

As the list indicates, depending on the participants and the situation, PE may use visual and dramatic forms of data collection more than other evaluation approaches. These methods often uncover important information that would not otherwise surface. The following story helps to illustrate the point.

*In an internal evaluation of a popular polio-prevention campaign in a remote area of the Atlantic Coast of Nicaragua, the health promoters from the various villages came together to reflect on their work. The planning meeting for the workshop included someone from the Ministry of Health, two doctors responsible for the area, and a Ministry-trained health promoter (a local person, recently literate). Another Canadian and I were participant observers in the process. During the planning meeting, an issue raised was that one of the village promoters had not arrived with his donkey to transport the vaccine. As a result of his lack of responsibility, the vaccine was rendered useless (given lack of refrigeration), and the villagers were not vaccinated. The doctors proposed that the man be rebuked publicly. The health promoter quietly disagreed. He suggested that he develop, with several other participants, a short skit to illustrate the problem. It would be used to generate discussion among participants about what had happened and what should be done. The skit was presented the next day. In addition to the problem of the man and his donkey, the drama also portrayed the arrogance of the doctors toward the local volunteers. Following the skit, the promoter who had failed to arrive with the donkey publicly acknowledged his mistake and apologized; he remained active (and responsible) in the malaria campaign that followed. The doctors reflected on their role, and suggestions were forthcoming as to how they might improve their relationship with the villagers.*

**Synthesizing, Analyzing, and Verifying the Data.** Data, once collected, are presented back to the participants by the evaluators for verification and collective analysis. This way of "socializing" the data is empowering for people who often realize for the first time that others share their perceptions and problems. In the process of collecting the data, new knowledge is usually generated as people correct and fill in gaps in information.

Data are verified in a number of ways at different stages in a PE process. Information is checked with key stakeholders as it is generated in workshop settings by writing the main points on a flip chart and constantly checking with participants to ensure accuracy. In this way, changes, additions, and deletions are made immediately. Reports of group meetings and workshops are transcribed and circulated to participants for their comments. The transcripts of individual interviews may be given to the individual for verification and amplification. This process is time-consuming when there are multiple interviews but is well worth the effort when time permits. Triangulation, mentioned earlier, is a good method for cross-checking data throughout the process.

Finally, most participatory processes include a feedback workshop with stakeholders to check and discuss proposed conclusions and recommendations. The evaluation team initially synthesizes the data, and the synthesis is presented to the participants along with questions and some tentative conclusions and recommendations. The ability to discuss initial findings and recommendations with key stakeholders is invaluable for testing the validity of the data, developing further analyses, and beginning work on an action plan.

**Developing Action Plans for the Future.** PE departs significantly from other approaches in assisting with the initial stages of action planning to address the recommendations of the evaluation. Possible areas for future work are discussed during the evaluation process, and some of the possibilities are presented to the key stakeholders in a feedback session. These possibilities are discussed, and broad action plans are developed for follow-up by the organization(s) involved.

**Controlling and Using Outcomes and Reports.** As mentioned in Chapter One, both strands of PE share an interest in seeing the evaluation results well used, in whatever form they take. For this purpose, it is essential that in the planning phase stakeholders make it clear how they wish to use the results and what form the report should take. Utilization approaches ask whether the evaluation report was used. PE also asks how it was used and for whose benefit (Pursley, 1996).

For evaluation reports to be of maximum benefit to the key stakeholders, several versions may be required. For example, one document may be prepared for funders while key stakeholders get a report that is also an organizing tool. For participants with low levels of literacy, visual tools, tapes, or workshop presentations may be used instead of written reports.

A critical issue in PE is control over the outcomes. Ideally, control remains in the hands of the key stakeholders. However, with a funder involved, a process of negotiation is likely to be needed, with the evaluator as mediator at the front end of the evaluation process. Without a prior understanding or agreement, problems can and do arise when the final report is being written. Here is one example.

*An external evaluator conducted a PE of a program in the United States in which urban young people were sent to work with isolated communities on specific projects. The key stakeholders involved (the young people and their community hosts) were both critical of the program, which tied the community funding to the placement of the young volunteers. The external evaluator, in her report to the funders, passed on these findings. However, for the funding agency, the placement of the young people was essential to the program, the "hook" they used for fundraising. As a result of the evaluation, all funding to those communities was terminated.*

The evaluator had failed to make the interests of all stakeholders transparent during the process. She had also failed to deal with the input from the communities in a strategic manner. When major stakeholder differences emerge at the end of the process, it is not always possible to negotiate terms that will benefit the key stakeholders.

## Conclusion

PE is a set of principles and a process, not a set of tools or techniques. Process is often seen as the poor cousin of content. However, in meeting the goals of PE, process is at least as important as the recommendations and results contained in the report. Through process participants develop ownership of the decisions made and develop new skills and confidence to improve their programs. We need to experiment with, document, and share efforts to develop approaches to evaluation that can help the people and programs our work is trying to support.

## References

Arnold, R., Burke, B., James, C., Martin, D., and Thomas, B. *Educating for a Change.* Toronto: Between the Lines and the Doris Marshall Institute, 1991.

Barndt, D. *Naming the Moment: Political Analysis for Action: A Manual for Community Groups.* Toronto: Jesuit Centre, 1989.

Chambers, R. *Whose Reality Counts? Putting the First Last.* London: Intermediate Technology Publications, 1997.

Ellis, D., Reid, G., and Barnsley, J. *Keeping on Track. An Evaluation Guide for Community Groups.* Vancouver: Women's Research Centre, 1990.

Feuerstein, M.-T. *Partners in Evaluation: Evaluating Development and Community Programmes with Participants.* London: Macmillan, 1986.

Freire, P. *Pedagogy of the Oppressed.* New York: Continuum, 1970.

Garaway, G. B. "Participatory Evaluation." *Studies in Educational Evaluation,* 1995, *21* (1), 85–102.

Greene, J. G. "Participatory Evaluation and the Evaluation of Social Programmes: Lessons Learned from the Field." Paper presented at the American Educational Research Association Conference, San Francisco, Apr. 16–20, 1986.

Hall, B., Etherington, A., and Jackson, T. "Evaluation, Participation and Community Health Care: Critiques and Lessons." Paper presented at the meeting of the American Health Association, Toronto, Nov. 1979.

Lather, P. "Research as Praxis." *Harvard Educational Review,* Aug. 1986, *56* (3), 257–277.

marino, d. *Wild Garden: Art, Education, and the Culture of Resistance.* Toronto: Between the Lines, 1997.

Preskill, H., and Caracelli, V. J. "The Past, Present and Future of Evaluation Use: Results from a Survey on Current Conceptions of Evaluation Use." Paper presented at the annual conference of the American Evaluation Association, Atlanta, Nov. 7, 1996.

Pursley, L. A. "Empowerment and Utilization Through Participatory Evaluation." Unpublished doctoral dissertation, Department of Human Service Studies, Cornell University, 1996.

Stuart, C. *Participatory Evaluation Methods: Course Manual*. Antigonish, Nova Scotia: Coady International Institute, 1994.

Sutherland, A. *Getting Everyone Involved: A Guide to Conducting Participatory Evaluations*. Calgary, Alberta: YWCA of Calgary and Zambia, 1995.

Tandon, R. *Participatory Evaluation: Issues and Concerns*. New Delhi: Society for Participatory Research in Asia, 1988.

United Nations Development Program (UNDP). *Who Are the Question Makers? A Participatory Evaluation Handbook*. New York: Office of Evaluation and Strategic Planning, United Nations Development Program, 1997.

Whitmore, E. "Participatory Approaches to Evaluation: Side Effects and Empowerment." Unpublished doctoral dissertation, Department of Human Service Studies, Cornell University, 1988.

BEVERLEY BURKE *is a writer and popular educator who has lived and worked in Africa and Latin America. She was cofounder of the Doris Marshall Institute for Education and Action in Toronto and now works in Ontario as a consultant to community organizations, trade unions, and international agencies.*

*The author examines three of her experiences with practical
participatory evaluation (or "meliorative participatory evaluation," as
she suggests) and reflects on what makes this approach work in
practice.*

# Making Sense of Participatory Evaluation Practice

*Jean A. King*

My first experience with participatory evaluation (PE) was a nightmare. A
newly hired high-ranking administrator in an urban school district, search-
ing for budget cuts, targeted an expensive curriculum-improvement program
known for its inefficiencies and questionable results. From his perspective, an
evaluation would provide information on whether the program—implemented in every secondary school in the district—worked and, more important, whether the program should continue, the infamous go/no-go decision.
The evaluator, the district's head of research and evaluation, asked me to be
part of an evaluation team that would make the best of a bad situation; the
team would work collaboratively with the teacher leaders who had been
pulled from their classrooms to train and support their colleagues in the program's mastery-learning techniques. Our goal as evaluators was clear: to identify the components of the program that were having a positive effect along
with those in need of improvement. By involving the teacher leaders in the
study, we would soften the evaluation experience, answer their questions
about the program, get meaningful first-hand information, and teach them
about the evaluation process to boot. Such a deal.

The disaster stemmed from our naive belief that someone might actually
be interested in the evaluation information. In retrospect it was fairly clear that
the administrator had decided to cut the program before the evaluation ever
began and that we were merely going through bureaucratic motions to justify
that decision. Our good intentions in working with the teachers who had the
most to lose from the program's demise surely paved the way to their professional hell. Despite hours of participation in the evaluation, when the program
was eliminated they lost their high hopes for student achievement as well as
their central-office positions. Our sincere promises that their involvement

would be of value were broken—through no fault of ours, but broken nevertheless (King, 1995).

The lesson was embarrassing and painful, but I learned well that participatory approaches to program evaluation bring different risks and challenges from those of the more traditional approaches with which I was familiar. Since that study, I have spent almost twenty years reflecting on these negatives along with the compelling positives that reinforce my commitment to involving others in the evaluation process. The purpose of this chapter is to compile these reflections along with brief case examples from my practice.

I must first, however, make a brief comment about terms. I was in graduate school during the emergent days of our field, and competing evaluation models appeared with regularity—Context, Input, Process, and Product (CIPP), discrepancy, democratic, goal-free, responsive. Dutiful student that I was, I memorized their differences and similarities for various qualifying examinations. The current explosion of participatory evaluation and participatory research labels reminds me of those days. We must now make sense of participatory evaluation, empowerment evaluation, various versions of action research (critical, collaborative, emancipatory, participatory), and so on. (I submit three labels for discussion, none of which has to my knowledge yet been claimed: open evaluation, evangelical free evaluation, and hypercritical action research.) Although professors may be relieved to again have myriad terms for quizzing students, the profusion of terms is surely an indication that participatory approaches to program evaluation are coming of age.

A glance at my curriculum vitae might cause you to wonder how I ever became attached to PE. Nothing in my graduate training points to it. I studied curriculum with a minor in measurement and educational research in an extremely traditional department of education. I took a sequence of statistics courses, critiqued countless quantitative research studies, conducted an empirical study of my own to demonstrate my quantitative mettle, and emerged, four years later, thoroughly grounded in a methodology for which I cared little. In retrospect—without knowing it at the time—I began to search for an inquiry process that combined what I had learned early on from my father (a school principal) about collaborating with people and using data, my 1960s commitment to social justice, and my formal training in measurement and quantitative methods. I read widely.

Over time I came to understand U.S. progressivism as two distinct approaches, each represented by a thriving stream of evaluation practice (Krueger and King, 1997). Conservative progressives emphasize social efficiency and accountability, seeking to solve social problems through scientific research that can be put into practice (for example, Edward Thorndike's intelligence testing, the use of efficiency experts, and large-scale policy studies). In contrast, liberal progressives frame their work with the ideal of social justice, seeking to democratize social processes by giving people voice and involving them in their own change. John Dewey and Jane Addams are early-twentieth-century examples, and many current approaches to PE spring from this tradition. My evaluation practice is clearly in the liberal tradition, built squarely on Dewey's pragmatic philosophy, which my father encouraged me to read, and on the neopragmatism that I regularly discuss with philosopher colleagues Dick Nunneley and Rob Orton (recently deceased) in an ongoing action-research study group.

My practice certainly falls under Cousins and Earl's 1992 definition of PE: "applied social research that involves trained evaluation personnel . . . *and* practice-based decision makers working in partnership" (emphasis in original). I label my work *collaborative action research* (King and Lonnquist, 1992), defined as "systematic inquiry by collaborative, self-critical communities, . . . a cyclic process that includes problem framing, planning, acting, observing, and reflecting in order to improve practice" (Nunneley, Orton, and King, 1997). Collaborative action research differs from a similar form of inquiry also labeled *action research* (*participatory action research* in the world of business and organizational development) that adheres more strictly to the canons of social science research. As a practitioner, however, I am not concerned with labels; what matters to me is the increasing ability of our field to learn from these approaches and to use them appropriately and effectively. To this end, this chapter comprises short case examples and my reflections on what I have learned from this work.

## Case Examples

The phrase *participatory evaluation* is for me a portmanteau word; as I noted earlier, I am perfectly willing to stretch its definition to cover a fairly broad range of my professional activities.

**Minneapolis Community Services (MCS) Project.** Since the mid-1980s, Minneapolis Community Services (a pseudonym), a social service agency created when several community centers merged, has had a mission to "help individuals and families . . . to strengthen their abilities, expand their opportunities, and change the conditions that limit their choices for the future." By 1994 six distinct neighborhood centers, supported by several cross-center programs (job training, early education, an annual citywide celebration), employed over two hundred people and struggled—like most not-for-profit nongovernmental organizations—to find ways to fund and evaluate their ongoing work. This project arose from the staff's dissatisfaction with traditional evaluation experiences, which had failed, in their minds, to fully capture the stories and real results of MCS. I was asked to collaborate in the development of a flexible evaluation system for the agency that would generate two types of information: (1) program-development information for staff, MCS board members, and, where appropriate, clients; and (2) accountability data for agency funders.

Over the course of 1995 three doctoral students from the University of Minnesota and I worked with MCS staff to create a PE process—under the label of action research—and to train staff members in its use. Central to the development of the project was the agency's executive director and the Action Research Facilitation (ARF) Committee. The ARF Committee began as a group of enthusiastic volunteers eager to escape the evaluation process then required and to create a replacement that would not only be easier but help them do better jobs. As a straightforward trial of the participatory process, the ARF Committee decided to examine the consistency of center hours across the city. They sent a survey to find out what hours each center was open on a daily basis. To the surprise of the committee, one center director—not on the ARF Committee—was outraged at what she perceived to be a direct intrusion on her administrative domain and refused to complete the simple form. Another questioned the origin of the survey but completed it. The remaining directors sent theirs in without comment, but the committee knew feathers had been ruffled.

Shortly after the survey incident, I was asked for the first time to attend a meeting of the MCS administrative team, ostensibly to present a progress report. When I arrived, the tension in the room was obvious. People who would normally greet me with cheery hellos avoided my eyes, and I was asked to sit in a seat facing a semicircle of chairs. After giving a short summary of our good intentions, I asked for questions. What followed was a verbal grilling far worse than any doctoral oral I have ever attended. Pointed questions and veiled accusations quickly revealed a within-agency power struggle, the executive director's commitment to the participatory approach, and managers' fears that the new evaluation system would take away too much of their control. The old system merely documented what employees and clients had done; the new data-based system had the potential to direct agency activities. Our mistaken assumption that it was sufficient to work with the executive director (who resigned shortly after this meeting) and the ARF Committee was readily apparent, and we immediately added all the managers or their representatives to an expanded ARF group for the duration of the development process.

Within six months, the evaluation team, working collaboratively with the broadened ARF Committee, generated two documents: (1) an introductory handout for new employees introducing them to the MCS action-research and evaluation process and (2) a notebook outlining how to conduct the process and containing materials and directions for a self-conducted training workshop. In the meantime, evaluation leaders at several centers conducted initial studies and finalized the forms they would submit to external agencies to meet requirements for outcome evaluation. At a culminating workshop, the ARF Committee leaders taught colleagues from all parts of the agency how to conduct MCS action research, passed out the new materials, and presented the results of their own projects.

**Thomas Paine Professional Practice School.** My involvement at this high school since 1990 has greatly influenced my thinking about PE approaches, particularly as I worked with colleagues on site to create a "learning organization" in an unlikely setting: an urban high school with an enrollment of 1,250 and a tough reputation. When I first entered the building, Paine (a pseudonym) was reputed to be the worst high school in the city—many students' attendance was irregular (as was their teachers'); student turnover was high; safety and racial tensions were ongoing concerns; academic achievement routinely placed the school at the bottom rank in the district; school pride was minimal at best; and teachers assigned to Paine transferred out as soon as they had rank. Thanks to the hard work of the Paine school community and the leadership of two principals and many teachers, however, Paine High School has turned itself around and is now a local success story.

Part of this success stems from ongoing collaborations: one with Paine's business partner, a local bank that sponsors a number of activities; and one with a nearby college of education that supports a Professional Development School (PDS) with school-based inquiry as a central goal. One principal sponsored and supported numerous evaluative efforts, believing that "people here have to get used to collecting data" (personal communication, Dec. 14, 1993) and "it's important not only to set a program up but also to evaluate it" (personal communication, Mar. 3, 1994). Two examples show the use of participatory approaches at Paine.

*Special Education Inclusion Study.* For two years (1993–1995) Paine's special education faculty participated in a collaborative study, funded by the state department of special education and facilitated by university personnel, of special education students mainstreamed into regular classes. First-year data pointed to the need for immediate and individualized counseling in the mainstream classroom if the students were to be successful there. In the second year, therefore, nine Paine teaching positions were cofunded using special education funding; this policy put special education expertise directly into classrooms and simultaneously allowed each teaching team in the building to release a teacher (all of whom were certified in special education) to serve as behavior dean. Those who formed the core of the evaluation team tracked data on the effects of these cofunded positions, and their personal interest virtually guaranteed that they would use the results. When the district's data seemed incorrect, those who kept records on individual students compiled a more accurate database for use in the following year.

*The Outcomes Accreditation (OA) Process.* The accrediting agency for schools in Paine's region supports a form of teacher-directed school assessment called Outcomes Accreditation. Paine has completed its first five-year cycle of this process (1992–1997). Using the district-mandated "building profile1/m," an extensive compilation of district data, 1/m faculty identified five OA target areas for the first year: respect, self-esteem, language arts, mathematics, and critical thinking. Not always in keeping with the OA time line, baseline data were eventually collected in all these areas during the second and third years; some of the data came from standardized tests, others from informal surveys, district records, and anecdotal information.

Student attendance and transience were major challenges to the school; at that time, 25 percent of the students might be absent on any given day; and the turnover rate was extremely high during the course of a year. Thus, the OA steering committee (a representative group of teachers) identified one targeted group of students to track over time: Paine students who attended school regularly and remained enrolled at Paine all four years. In the third and fourth years, teachers developed and implemented interventions in each of the targeted areas (for example, they created remedial language-arts instruction for those identified as most in need; they eliminated tracking in ninth- and tenth-grade math classes). In the fifth year, teachers again collected data and compared them with the baseline data. This was a serious accountability process; Paine received North Central accreditation because data pointed to improvement in four of the five target areas, and the OA process resumed with a second five-year cycle.

**Bush Educators' Program (BEP).** Since the mid-1970s, three Bush Foundation–funded leadership-development programs for school administrators have been a source of in-service administrative training for a select group of Minnesota educators. A revision resulted in the Bush Educators' Program, which is designed for twenty-four educators per year who serve in many roles, including central-office and building administrators, classroom teachers and specialists, and state education department personnel.

Involving a six-week commitment over two years, the BEP curriculum emphasizes the importance of problem framing, cross-role team building, and collaboration for long-term change. The program has three phases:

I. An overview of key issues in educational change coupled with extensive personal assessment

II. An intensive experience in one district where BEP participants serve as external data collectors on a major change issue

III. Individual projects designed to result in meaningful change in participants' own districts

Along with other university faculty, I have a role that begins with Phase II and is twofold. First, we teach people the skills of evaluation (how to conduct focus-group surveys, telephone surveys, individual interviews, large group interventions) while we collectively conduct a study for a volunteer district (Owatonna in 1996, Milaca in 1997, and St. Paul in 1998). Second, we require BEP participants to envision and implement their own projects. These not only tackle a central change issue (K–12 curriculum articulation, birth–12 literacy instruction, standards-based reform) but also provide data to document the results for both adults and students. Every project must pay attention to student achievement in some form. In 1998, with the third BEP group in progress, there were close to seventy such projects across Minnesota. I work to coach and support participants as they implement these change projects, which are by their nature collaborative action-research efforts—PEs by BEP participants and their teams.

## What Makes This Approach Work in Practice

In King (1995), I presented examples of participatory studies and what I had learned from them. My experiences since then have generated a baker's half dozen lessons: two of my earlier observations reaffirmed, two revised, and three additional lessons learned. Many of these reflect what colleagues (Yoland Wadsworth and Michael Patton, for example) have also discussed, and while these lessons may not seem profound, oftentimes the simplest ideas are those most difficult to bring to life.

*Participatory evaluation efforts require high levels of interpersonal and organizational trust.* Although trust is certainly not sufficient and in no way guarantees the success of a collaborative evaluation study, it is surely necessary. Two BEP projects took place in school settings where the participants' immediate supervisors—rightly or wrongly—questioned their intentions. Such skepticism would have ensured failure, and so time had to be spent integrating the administrators' concerns into the framing of issues. Other examples come from projects within the new MCS system. At one community center, a small number of committed practitioners took a collective leap of faith, designed a door-to-door and in-center survey to assess factors that limited community involvement, and used the results to organize a neighborhood clean-up effort. At another center, people devoted their energies to arguing about why MCS wanted the new evaluation system, who was going to make the process happen, and how they could best get around it. Their lack of trust led to little action beyond complaints.

*People taking part in PE efforts must create shared meaning of their experiences over time.* Time-consuming as they may be, communication and interactive discussion are central components of participatory studies that work. Like trust, the development of shared meaning is necessary but not sufficient for the process to work. For example, one BEP project that was studying grade configuration across a district changed dramatically when the group sat down to analyze data and discovered that their survey results were in direct conflict with what people had said in focus groups. Creating shared meaning of the conflicting data forced people to generate a lengthy list of possible reasons for the difference and stimulated the project's next steps. Participants suddenly became interested in what their data meant and what they might do about a situation they once thought they had understood. When people perceive evaluation information as interesting or even provocative, they become energized.

*PE efforts must address the power structure within which they are working.* Until recently I sought out settings where I believed the political context would support a participatory project, regardless of the organizational structure. My experiences that awful afternoon at the MCS administrative team meeting showed me the problem with this approach. Regardless of how well-intentioned some—or even most—people may be, to the extent that an organizational structure remains hierarchical, it may be difficult for PE processes to take root. Managers in a traditional hierarchy are responsible for activities in their domain, and it may be unfair to simultaneously ask them to relinquish control and to remain responsible. In such settings, top managers must provide ongoing and extremely visible support in a number of ways—for example, by modeling the process in cross-agency participatory projects in which they truly relinquish control, by providing incentives like release time during business hours, by showing up at training sessions and discussions, and by publicly celebrating the process's results. Even with such support, however, the danger remains that the PE process can be cut off by administrative fiat.

I now not only pay attention to organizational politics but, to the extent that I have any influence (and it's important to note that I often don't), I also work to change them in support of participatory processes. Although this form of advocacy surely smacks of "transformative" work, the difference is that I do not assume that what a colleague calls the "life of E's"—empowerment, enlightenment, and emancipation (Nunneley, 1997)—will necessarily follow from my efforts. In the absence of direct attention to organizational (as opposed to societal) politics, I worry that use-oriented participatory approaches to evaluation merely improve on the decision-making model that has been prevalent in the field since the early 1970s.

*Not only do PE processes require volunteers; they require leaders.* In the best of all possible worlds, people would volunteer to participate in studies. However, as I have noted, you can lead people to evaluation, but you cannot make them participate (King, 1995). I have also learned that it is not enough to have volunteers. You also need leaders who can attract or recruit people to the evaluation process, who are eager to learn and facilitate the process, who will serve as idea champions, and who are willing to stay the course when things go wrong—as they inevitably do. In each of the cases discussed above, examples of gifted and charismatic leaders shine brightly: the community-center head who spearheaded an evaluation and eventually assumed leadership of the ARF Committee; the youthful teacher who emerged as the natural choice to lead the second cycle of the OA process; the high school teacher on special assignment whose Bush project has mobilized an entire community to address early-childhood literacy issues. In the absence of such individuals, PE cannot succeed.

*PE processes are best done slowly.* I routinely quote Mae West's famous line "anything worth doing is worth doing slowly" because, in my experience, you cannot rush participatory processes. People simply need time to build or reaffirm relationships and trust, to identify issues that matter, to learn about evaluation methodologies, to collect data, to collectively make sense of them—and to do all this while they are typically working full-time at their "regular" jobs. To rush the process may well destroy it.

*Two incentives are key to fostering PE processes: tackling important issues and having appropriate resources.* My experience suggests that volunteers studying a burning issue will work long and hard on PEs. If their organization can also meet some accountability requirement (as in the MCS case) or can receive accreditation (as in the Paine case) or if an individual can be recognized for leadership (as in the BEP case), better yet. Not surprisingly, my experience also suggests the need for individual incentives—stipends and honoraria if these are available, recognition within the organization, and, especially, time during the day while people learn to integrate the evaluation process into their ongoing work.

*Outside facilitators of the PE process have an important role.* A graduate student once asked me, "If action research can only be done on your own organization, what exactly is it that you do when you work with people on such processes?" I have labeled this issue the dilemma of facilitation: on the one hand, if you, as an outsider, facilitate the PE process, you may directly affect its outcome; on the other hand, if you do not facilitate it, the process may well die (King, 1994). Although the dilemma remains, I now see a viable role that facilitators can play in fostering PE processes. First, they provide an outsider's perspective as part of the reflection process and therefore may see matters in a different and helpful way. Second, they unavoidably represent the broader world of evaluation and can bring to bear their technical skills. Third, as individuals they may serve as potential scapegoats—as I almost did in the MCS project—or as positive supporters, saying, "You're doing fine," and validating people's evaluation work. These are not trivial activities, and people interested in facilitating participatory processes can learn them.

## Final Thoughts

Although I taught junior high school English for six years, I did not remain a classroom teacher, nor did I become a community organizer or a social worker. I lead a life that is largely separate from the poor and alienated of our society. I no longer believe that idealized versions of society are possible, except in poetry or as rhetorical placeholders. Instead, I am an evaluator committed to fostering PE processes among those who work in schools and social service agencies because my experience has only reinforced my sense of how alien formal evaluation processes often seem to those outside the field. My commitment to pragmatism, first borrowed from my father, suggests that it does not have to be that way, and I now work for and welcome any real progress in existing institutions.

So what is my brand of PE? Like my colleague and literal neighbor Michael Quinn Patton (we live a mile apart in St. Paul), I routinely question how people will use the information created in the evaluation process, which places me, to use Cousins and Whitmore's (Chapter One) scheme, in the "practical" ("utilization") category of participatory evaluators. I do seek a "balanced" approach to control of the evaluation process, although my commitment to collaborative action research suggests this as a beginning stage to eventual capacity building within a school or agency. I do work with "primary users" and do not attempt to connect with "all legitimate groups." I do encourage "extensive participation in all phases of the evaluation." What is missing in that categorization, however, is my ongoing and primary commitment to improving social institutions. My approach is not "mere" technical problem solving or decision making. American pragmatists' approaches stem by nature from social meliorism, and to ignore their meliorism is to misrepresent their intention. (Dewey, for example, surely valued problem solving, but his philosophy without exception places it within the context of ultimately creating a more democratic society.) Perhaps my approach can best be labeled *meliorative participatory evaluation,* halfway on a continuum between participatory and transformative.

How does my work relate to more explicitly labeled "emancipatory" or "empowerment" approaches? I worry greatly that some theorists have chosen wonderful words without fully accepting their theoretical underpinnings. These underpinnings are routinely attributed to the writings of Edmund Husserl or Jürgen Habermas, both hefty philosophical works in German or in translation. Although sharing an impatience with the intransigence of social institutions, I nevertheless reject the claims of critical theorists who claim that the teachers, administrators, and social service staff with whom I work are "duped" and "deluded" and that our joint efforts must necessarily help them see what they as theorists already know—that is (and I am paraphrasing), that a veil of tradition prevents people from seeing the essential reality of the world (Carr and Kemmis, 1992; Van Manen, 1990; McTaggart, 1991).

Quite the opposite is true. I believe that not only are the people I collaborate with not duped, but they alone can really make sense of their work in context. Given my liberal progressive bent, I choose to work within existing institutions, typically small ones, and to work collaboratively to effect social justice through building the capacity of individuals within these institutions to engage in meaningful inquiry and change. To those who would fault me for not working directly with the "clients" of social institutions (the "oppressed"), I point to what philosophers might call a category error; I have chosen simply to work elsewhere and would invite critics to examine the work I do, as opposed to the work I do not do.

At the same time I am troubled by the pleasant life I lead and the articles I write so glibly. The deaths of Princess Diana and Mother Teresa—both committed to social change, but enacting their beliefs so differently—provide an apt image for my concern. I fear I am the Princess Diana of PE—committed to social justice but employed at a research university where I am rewarded for my academic writing, living in the ivory tower with regular forays into the "real world" of practice, a middle-class mom who drives her children to music lessons. The Mother Teresas of PE do not write articles about their work. They wear the North American equivalent of one-dollar saris, live in run-down neighborhoods, make little money, and work directly with the people who are poorly served by our society. Although the question of motives is particularly difficult, if we truly want to change the world, should we not—as literary theorist Stanley Fish suggests—just do it, rather than evaluating it (1995)?

### References

Carr, W., and Kemmis, S. *Becoming Critical: Education, Knowledge and Action Research.* London: Falmer, 1992.

Cousins, J. B., and Earl, L. M. "The Case for Participatory Evaluation." *Educational Evaluation and Policy Analysis,* 1992, *14* (4), 397–418.

Fish, S. *Professional Correctness.* Oxford: Clarendon Press, 1995.

King, J. A. "Review of *Action Research: A Short Modern History* by R. McTaggart." *Journal of Curriculum Studies,* 1994, 6 (4), 465.

King, J. A. "How Viable Is Participatory Evaluation in School Settings?" In J. B. Cousins and L. M. Earl (eds.), *Participatory Evaluation.* London: Falmer, 1995.

King, J. A., and Lonnquist, M. P. *A Review of Writing on Action Research: 1944–Present.* Minneapolis: Center for Applied Research and Educational Improvement, 1994.

Krueger, R. A., and King, J. A. *Involving Community Members in Focus Groups.* Thousand Oaks, Calif.: Sage, 1997.

McTaggart, R. *Action Research: A Short Modern History.* Geelong, Victoria, Australia: Deakin University Press, 1991.

Nunneley, R. D., Jr. "Inquiry, Practice, Consequence: Educational Action Research and the Neopragmatist Spirit." Unpublished doctoral dissertation, University of Minnesota, 1997.

Nunneley, R. D., Jr., Orton, R. E., and King, J. A. "Validating Standards for Action Research." Paper presented at the annual meeting of the American Educational Research Association, Chicago, Mar. 1997.

Patton, M. Q. *Utilization-Focused Evaluation.* (3rd ed.) Thousand Oaks, Calif.: Sage, 1997.

Van Manen, M. *Researching the Lived Experience.* London, Ontario: University of Western Ontario, 1990.

JEAN A. KING *is associate professor in the College of Education and Human Development, University of Minnesota. She is the former director of the Center for Applied Research and Educational Improvement. Her research interests include long-term school change, participatory evaluation, and evaluation use.*

*Haitian staff members of nongovernmental organizations are trained in participatory evaluation methodology and then apply their training in facilitating the evaluation of fifteen grassroots projects. This case study reviews the lessons learned, the key outcomes, and some limitations of the process.*

# A Case Study of Participatory Evaluation in Haiti

*Françoise P. Coupal, Marie Simoneau*

This case study describes a participatory evaluation (PE) undertaken in Haiti in April 1997. The evaluation framework and its implementation were built from the ground up, with the involvement of key project stakeholders in all phases of the evaluation, from planning to training and implementation. Given the specific international-development context, this model may differ from others. However, we hope that this example will shed light on the particular approaches, resources, and skills required to undertake a successful participatory evaluation.

## Background

Haiti, which shares the western third of the island of Hispaniola with the Dominican Republic, is the poorest country in the Western Hemisphere. The history of Haiti is one of sharply opposing interests and competing visions of state and nation. Since Haiti declared its independence in 1804, it has been ruled by two powerful groups: military leaders and a merchant oligarchy. The vast majority of Haitians have been systematically excluded from meaningful participation in the development of their country. Their life experiences are determined largely by favoritism, corruption, arbitrariness, violence, and repression.

In 1990, the first democratic election in the history of Haiti brought Jean-Bertrand Aristide to power. Within months, however, he was overthrown in a military coup, leading to years of violence and terror. With the U.S. invasion and return of President Aristide in 1994, nongovernmental organizations (NGOs) and grassroots organizations began to rebuild Haitian civil society and to implement development programs. Severe economic, social, and political problems remain, however, exacerbated by the imposition of a strict structural-adjustment program that has narrowed the role of the state in addressing these issues.

Within this particularly troubled political, economic, and social milieu, the Canada-Haiti Humanitarian Alliance Fund was set up in 1993 by the Canadian Council for International Cooperation (CCIC). Sponsored by the Canadian International Development Agency, the Canada-Haiti Humanitarian Alliance Fund was seen as a mechanism for supporting the work of local NGOs within civil society during a period of political instability and severe repression. Thirty-six projects were funded in various sectors, including agriculture and reforestation, health and nutrition, sanitation, credit, institutional strengthening, street children, and communications.

In evaluating the impact of its efforts, CCIC wanted to go beyond the accountability function to build capacity among Haitian and Canadian NGOs by training local stakeholders in participatory approaches and methodology. The agency viewed the evaluation itself as a learning process and a way of examining projects to determine how they could be made more effective. The evaluation would also allow CCIC to assess the efficiency and the impacts of the fund.

These were the main challenges faced in planning the PE:

- The integration of new methods despite the limited time and resources accorded to the evaluation
- The coordination of more than thirty-six projects and forty Canadian and Haitian partners dispersed over four disparate regions
- The lack of linkages among these projects
- The broad range of NGO activities
- The variation in cost of the projects—from less than CDN$5,000 to more than CDN$250,000
- Having the NGOs available and able to participate in three weeks of intense training and evaluation
- Choosing appropriate program staff for training
- The timelines of the projects (some of the projects had been completed; others were still in progress)
- Cultural and language barriers (Creole is the first language of Haitians, making the translation of materials into both French and Creole a necessity)
- The possibility that some program staff might feel threatened by the evaluation process
- The lack of Haitian cofacilitators familiar with participatory methods

Given these challenges, the preparatory and training phases of the evaluation were crucial to its eventual success.

## Salient Features of the Participatory Evaluation

The evaluation had the following (specific) features:

- Fifteen projects were evaluated over a three-week period with teams of three to five persons per project.

- The selection of projects and the themes were determined in a planning meeting with project stakeholders.
- Twenty-eight participants were drawn from NGOs directly linked to the projects and trained to become PE facilitators.
- Efforts were made from the outset to achieve gender balance among the participants.
- Intense training over four days with daily practice within the community was essential to the learning process. The residential training took place in a rural setting.
- The facilitators were project stakeholders involved in the collective reflection and discussion of the project's achievements.
- Facilitators were not directly involved in the evaluation of their own projects.
- When participants for training in PE methods were selected, openness and willingness to learn new methods were deemed more important than a given level of education or prior experience.

## Overall Framework of the Evaluation

Although the initial impetus for review came from the funder, the final decisions as to the type and scope of the evaluation rested with project stakeholders attending an initial planning meeting. The funder fully supported the iterative development of a framework based on feedback from the Haitian partners. As the evaluator-trainers, we undertook two missions in Haiti: to plan and "flesh out" a framework for the participatory evaluation and to focus on training and the launching of the evaluation. One can distinguish four key process phases: planning, training, visiting project sites, and collectively reflecting on and disseminating the findings.

Phase I: The Planning Mission. A one-week mission took place in February 1997 to plan the evaluation. A first meeting was held with directors or program staff of thirty-six NGOs and several community representatives. Participants were initiated into the world of PE through a series of exercises used throughout the day. This process created an atmosphere of enthusiasm and intrigue, as the Haitians were accustomed to traditional meetings and presentations.

The planning meeting sought to answer some key questions:

- Why were we undertaking an evaluation and what were its objectives?
- What indicators should be used?
- Was there a commitment to undertake a PE?
- If so, what resources and support could be expected from the local NGOs?
- In terms of profile and skills, who should be involved in the evaluation?
- When should the evaluation take place?
- Where should the training take place?

In an initial exercise, small groups were asked to discuss and draw pictures of their experiences of evaluation. That this exercise proved revealing can be seen from Figures 5.1 and 5.2. In Figure 5.1, a well-dressed evaluator sits behind a desk with file drawers full of reports. The project stakeholders are outside, in the community. Arrows indicate the flow of information. The "expert" may write a report for the donor, but the project stakeholders are clearly the objects of evaluation.

In Figure 5.2, which depicts PE, all the project stakeholders are meeting in one corner. Then, the group goes into the community to meet project beneficiaries, individually or in small groups, under a tree or at a workplace. One person who helped draw the picture explained, "There is an exchange of ideas, experiences, and a group discussion of the problems and solutions. The results are shared with all key stakeholders."

The drawings helped to focus discussion on the type of evaluation NGOs preferred: a traditional evaluation, where a team of "experts" is sent in, or a participatory process, involving project stakeholders in a process of collective reflection and analysis.

Projects were selected by pulling names out of a hat. The names were then entered onto a matrix to ensure a sample that represented projects different in size, geographic region, and sectoral focus.

Participants were then asked to define three issues that they would like the evaluation to examine. Each response was placed on a colored Post-it Note, and the responses were then grouped thematically by the participants themselves. These preliminary themes, which guided the evaluation exercise, included the impact of the project, its sustainability and viability, gender equity, and the project's relationship with the community and other NGO partners.

Also discussed at the meeting were the time line for evaluation and the level of commitment one could expect from different stakeholders. Commit-

**Figure 5.1.  Traditional Method of Evaluation**

**Figure 5.2.  Participatory Evaluation**

ment could be demonstrated, for example, by providing transportation and accommodations during the evaluation or by participating in the training and evaluation phases. The purposes of this approach and these exercises were to demystify the process of evaluation and to ensure an early buy-in and interested commitment to it.

The results of this planning meeting were shared with all the Canadian and Haitian NGOs, and they were asked to contribute. Those who could not take part in the training phase were encouraged to participate in the final "restitution," a half-day meeting where the results of project evaluations and an assessment by participants would be exchanged.

**Phase II: Training Participants.**  Twenty-eight participants were trained to be "PE facilitators" by two trainers (the authors) using Participatory Rural Appraisal (PRA), also known as Participatory Learning and Action (PLA). These approaches use visual tools and local materials (rocks, stones, seeds, beans) to generate discussion among and analysis by participants.

The four-day workshop was entirely experiential, and exercises were designed to stimulate learning about PE and the key concepts and tools of participation. Exercises involved skits, role playing, sorting exercises, drawings, small-group discussions, and hands-on exercises such as matrices, ranking, community mapping, force-field analysis, historical time lines, gender division of labor, and transect walks. Some examples follow.

To help participants understand the difference between participatory and traditional evaluations, short descriptions of each approach were written on individual strips of paper: "donor control of resources and decisions," "control and decisions by program/project beneficiary," "collective learning process," "an extractive process, outsider's perspective," "stakeholders are the question makers." Thirty strips of paper were distributed to each group. The statements were then discussed within the group and sorted into two categories: participatory or traditional evaluation. Similar exercises were done using open and closed questions followed by mock interviews.

Role playing was used in a number of exercises to make participants aware of how certain attitudes and behaviors can have an adverse effect on others. Groups of three participants acted as dominators, the dominated, listeners, and even as saboteurs. Discussion followed as to how it felt to be dominated or sabotaged, and strategies for neutralizing dominators and saboteurs were addressed. These exercises are excellent energizers and make participants aware of social dynamics and class differences. Those who dominate often have a higher level of education, social standing, or prestige and tend to prevent poorer participants from speaking for themselves. It is essential for a facilitator to spot dominators and saboteurs early on and to ensure that evaluation findings are not skewed in their favor.

Mapping involves asking community members to "map" their community from a local perspective. Often what goes unmentioned by participants can be as important as what they note on this map. Community members may also highlight key areas of project activity or distinguish different socioeconomic groupings. Mapping is an excellent tool to use when first arriving in a community and can provide an important insiders' perspective.

Exercises such as these, combined with daily excursions into the community, gave participants the experience necessary to become PE facilitators.

Another exercise was to explore collectively the attitudes and personal qualities of a facilitator; this exercise was important because facilitators play a critical role in creating a climate of trust in the community. The characteristics of a good facilitator include an open mind, being a good listener, allowing others to speak, patience, trust in people's abilities, and valuing the opinions of others. Role playing and practical exercises in the community setting enabled participants to develop their facilitation skills.

Often, PRA uses a stick or a marker to draw visual representations. The question of who holds the stick is quite significant, as it is representationally akin to holding power. "Handing over the stick" thus has tremendous symbolic value in participatory methods.

Early in the training, a key obstacle was the belief of PE facilitators that poor or illiterate people could not map their community or make matrices for themselves. The facilitators tended to guard the stick or marker and acted as interpreters rather than letting the people themselves use the tools. Resistance to handing over the stick was particularly strong during the first few days of training but diminished over time, as facilitators gained confidence and realized, to their surprise, that poor people could in fact participate quite effectively. Trainers also stressed the need for participants to work on their own internal blocks and areas of resistance.

**Phase III: Visits to Projects.** The PE facilitators visited fifteen projects over a two-week period. Each facilitator visited two projects and spent three days living on the project site. The group of twenty-eight facilitators divided into teams of three to five persons, composed to ensure gender balance, openness, facility with the methods, and expertise in the project area.

Each team had a number of evaluation issues to explore with the community, such as the impact of the project, its relationship with other partners (CCIC, NGOs, the community), sustainability and viability, efficiency, management, the role of women, and gender equity. A number of subquestions were devised by the participants for each of the overall themes.

**Phase IV: Collective Reflection and Dissemination.** Each team was responsible for consolidating its community work into a brief project report. Each report summarized the key findings, integrating the maps and drawings done by community people. If drawings had been made on the ground, the team replicated them on paper. At the end of their visit, some teams debriefed project stakeholders in the community to check the reliability of their findings. Each team was also responsible for making a presentation of their findings to the larger group of PE facilitators. These presentations were an important source of mutual education, given the active exchange of learning experiences.

All the program partners were invited to attend a final presentation organized by the PE facilitators. It involved presenting the drawings, maps, and findings of each project evaluated, role playing, and providing testimonials of their experiences.

## Key Outcomes and Findings

The evaluation generated a number of important outcomes at various levels.

**Undertaking PE.** The trainers learned the following practical lessons about PE:

- Excellent logistical and administrative support are essential.
- Allowing sufficient down time (two days) at the end of project visits for group reflection and lessons learned is necessary.
- Ensuring a good gender mix is critical to the evaluation process.
- Some learners take longer than others, and special assistance may be required to help them overcome their internal and cultural blocks.
- Training outside of the capital city in modest surroundings can contribute significantly to developing a team and learning to adapt to different living conditions.
- External evaluators should "walk the talk" and promote cultural sensitivity and good participatory practices (by eating local food, sleeping on mats, handing over the stick, listening to others).
- The process should not be rushed. Some of the best interviews are those where one takes time to build trust and rapport.

The facilitators also learned a number of lessons from their first practical exercises in the community:

- It is essential to use the tools and adapt them to conversations rather than simply mechanically practicing them.
- The initial strategy for approaching community members is critical, as individuals' trust must be earned before they are presented with the tools.
- In a rural area, physical contact or position can be more important than eye contact because peasants do not tend to look each other in the eye.
- Having people of both genders available for interviews is important. It is harder to use PRA methods with women because they are busy.

**Building Capacity.** One of the key outcomes of the evaluation process was the building of capacity. At a personal level, the trainees were transformed; their outlook on poor people had changed significantly. The facilitators had become much more aware of the constraints that poor people face and of the ways they are subjugated. The facilitators' understanding and appreciation of qualitative methods and of the importance of living in the community were also sharpened. One commented, "I was able to discover with these tools that everyone has the potential, and it is at that moment that one realizes the capacity and potential of community members." Another realized that "from the cultural perspective the community taught me many things." (For elaboration, see Coupal, 1997, pp. 11–12.)

Although training laid the foundation for the PE process, the real growth took place during daily excursions into the community and during visits to the projects. There the PE facilitators realized the importance of gaining trust and establishing rapport before introducing tools or asking questions. They also learned that community members were quite capable of using matrices and making maps. However, the impact of the facilitators on the community was more difficult to gauge. Certainly there was a great deal of curiosity and intrigue during these team visits to the projects. Some project beneficiaries felt a strong sense of ownership of their drawings and adorned the walls of their offices with them.

The learning curve was evident. On Day 1, the facilitators were interested in PE methods but skeptical that they could be applied in the Haitian context. They felt that illiterate people in the communities would not be capable of using the tools effectively. By Day 16, having visited the projects and successfully engaged community people in the evaluation process, the PE facilitators had completely changed their attitudes. One summed it up by saying, "The real danger to development is literate people who are not aware."

**Data Interpretation and Presentation.** Data were interpreted at three points: after the first series of project visits, after the second series of project visits, and during a final presentation open to all Fund partners. Each team was also responsible for communicating the results to the community they had visited before leaving, although all did not do so. Over time, there was a distinct improvement in the quality of the presentations. Increasing emphasis was placed on the evaluation themes rather than on the tools used. There was also increased mastery of the general approach, of asking open-ended questions, and of addressing sometimes delicate themes.

**Findings Regarding the Program.** As noted earlier, the projects being evaluated covered a wide range of sectors. It was estimated that over ten thousand persons benefited from the Fund's program. Some projects provided support to grassroots groups of two hundred people or more, which allowed the Fund to expand its coverage significantly. Because the program was established at a critical juncture in Haiti's political development, it also created opportunities for local groups to come together and organize. (See Coupal, 1997, for full details.)

The PE facilitators felt strongly that successful projects were those that integrated participation throughout the project cycle, and that projects without participation had a limited impact on the community. The evaluation also noted the importance of networking and cross-fertilization when stakeholders are brought together to discuss issues of common interest and concern.

**Limitations and Difficulties.** In order to be effective, participatory approaches must be both inherent in the NGO's programming and an organic component of project design. Many of the projects evaluated in this study were neither designed nor implemented in a participatory way. We hope that these PE results will be used to refine key issues and generate new questions to be addressed in the next phase of the projects.

One crucial limitation of this evaluation was the absence of some key stakeholders. Even though project partners were informed in advance of the evaluation and asked to facilitate the work of the PE teams, some of these stakeholders were unable or unwilling to comply. Certainly more than one field visit needs to be made, and more coordination before visits is essential in order to guarantee the involvement of all stakeholders. Additional time should be allocated to field visits and to the consolidation of findings.

In preparing for the evaluation, we discovered that local expertise in PRA/PLA was nonexistent in Haiti. In addition, the quality of the teams of PE facilitators varied enormously. This discrepancy was reflected in the unevenness of the evaluation reports, especially in the first phase, when participants were learning and applying the tools.

## Conclusion

The Haitian experience revealed that PEs are a viable alternative to traditional approaches to evaluation. Arguments against the use of PE include time and cost, the necessity for projects evaluated to be designed in a participatory manner, and the belief that participants cannot "objectively" evaluate projects (Chambers, 1993; Tandon and Fernandes, 1988a, 1988b; United Nations Development Program, 1997). This case study addresses some of these concerns. The Fund was designed in a traditional way to respond to donor priorities and initiatives. Although there was some stakeholder consultation, the design and implementation of individual projects varied enormously, and some projects were not explicitly participatory. Introducing a participatory approach to evaluation did not disrupt the implementation of the projects. On the contrary, the PE facilitators were able to appreciate more fully the importance of stakeholder participation in all aspects of a project's implementation. As well, project stakeholders themselves (the community people) became quite interested in the methods and tools used.

Although the cost of this evaluation (around US$65,000) is comparable to that of traditional evaluations, its impact on the PE facilitators was certainly greater than a traditional evaluation would have been, at both a personal and a professional level. This experience changed the way the PE facilitators viewed development. The time (three weeks) required to undertake this evaluation was comparable to the time required for traditional evaluations and possibly was shorter given the number and complexity of the projects. One advantage in this PE was the large number of facilitators, which enabled us to cover a large number of projects in a short period of time.

This evaluation demonstrated that evaluations do not require outside "experts"; a core team of experienced and skilled practitioners can effectively train others to use and apply participatory methods to evaluations.

The PE facilitators have now formed their own network to continue using participatory methods, to exchange experiences, and to support and encourage one another. The experience created a unique bond among them. As many of these facilitators work for different NGOs, they have also become important points for contact and exchange. The network has met on a regular basis since the evaluation; some are also interested in sharing their knowledge with other organizations.

Many have integrated PE tools into their day-to-day work with organizations and communities. Facilitators now have an understanding of what is meant by sustainability and viability, which has helped them in discussions with donors.

Finally, a number of challenges lie ahead. Will the newly formed participatory network enable these new practitioners to continue to learn through action and debate, to hone their skills and deepen understanding? Have their behaviors and attitudes changed in a meaningful and lasting way? Will the tools be used to empower local people and give them a say in projects affecting them, and can they make decisions that will influence other stakeholders? Will they be able to address underlying issues in their communities? If even some of these objectives are attained, this evaluation will have succeeded in building PRA/PLA capacity among NGOs in Haiti and, through them, in beginning a process of empowering their constituents, the poor and the weak.

### References

Chambers, R. "Shortcut Methods for Gathering Social Information for Rural Development Projects." In M. Cernea (ed.), *Putting People First.* Oxford: Oxford University Press, 1993.
Chambers, R. "Participatory Rural Appraisal (PRA): Analysis of Experience." *World Development,* 1994, 22 (9), 1253–1268.

Coupal, F. "Participatory Evaluation of the Canadian Haitian Humanitarian Alliance Fund, Final Report, July 1997. Haiti." Report submitted to the Canadian Council for International Cooperation, Ottawa, July 1997.

Feuerstein, M.-T. *Partners in Evaluation: Evaluating Development and Community Programmes with Participants.* London: Macmillan, 1986.

Feuerstein, M.-T. "Finding the Methods to Fit the People: Training for Participatory Evaluation." *Community Development Journal,* 1988, *23,* 16–25.

Freedman, J. *Participatory Evaluations: Making Projects Work.* Technical Paper TP94/2. Calgary, Alberta: Division of International Development, International Centre, University of Calgary, 1994.

Narayan-Parker, D. *Participatory Evaluation: Tools for Managing Change in Water and Sanitation.* World Bank Technical Paper 207. Washington, D.C.: World Bank, 1993.

Tandon, R., and Fernandes, W. *Participatory Evaluation: Issues and Concerns.* New Delhi: Society for Participatory Research in India, 1988a.

Tandon, R., and Fernandes, W. *Report of the International Forum on Participatory Evaluation, New Delhi, 1–5 March 1988.* New Delhi: Society for Participatory Research in Asia, 1988b.

United Nations Development Program. *Who Are the Question Makers? A Participatory Evaluation Handbook.* New York: Office of Evaluation and Strategic Planning, United Nations Development Program, 1997.

*FRANÇOISE P. COUPAL is director of Mosaic.net International Inc., a consulting firm in international development headquartered in Ottawa, Canada. In addition to having over 15 years of experience in development, she is an experienced participatory evaluator and facilitator in participatory methods.*

*MARIE SIMONEAU has more than 15 years of work experience in the coordination and management of international development programs, as both an NGO staff person and volunteer board member. She is currently directing an environmental management training program in Jordan for the University Service of Canada.*

*This chapter provides a detailed case study of participatory evaluation in a large-scale community-revitalization program, using grassroots "citizen learning teams" to monitor and track progress. Lessons and implications for scaling up participatory evaluation in government programs are discussed.*

# Scaling Up: Participatory Monitoring and Evaluation of a Federal Empowerment Program

John Gaventa, Victoria Creed, Janice Morrissey

Around the world, participatory methods have been used in the monitoring and evaluation of development initiatives for over two decades, especially at the project level (Estrella and Gaventa, 1998). Despite this international experience, participatory monitoring and evaluation are less widely promoted in the United States, especially in the context of government programs or initiatives.

There are precedents however. In the community-development field, one historical example may be found in the work done by the Center for Community Change in the early 1970s to train citizen teams to monitor the use and

---

*Note:* Portions of this chapter are drawn from *Findings and Recommendations of the Community Partnership Center EZ/EC Learning Initiative,* prepared by the Community Partnership Center, University of Tennessee, with funding support from the Ford Foundation and the United States Department of Agriculture, Co-operative Agreement 43–3AEN–4–80101. Our thanks to all of the learning-team leaders, researchers, and project participants whose work we are reporting on here. However, the findings and conclusions represent the opinions of the authors and are not necessarily those of the project participants or funding agencies.

The regional researchers on the project included Milan Wall and Troy Gagner, Heartland Center for Leadership Development; Timothy Collings, University of Kentucky; Ntam Baharanyi and Henry Findlay, Tuskegee University; Cruz Torres, University of Texas–Pan American; Helen Lewis, Highlander Center; and Pamela D. Moore, Greenville, Mississippi.

The sites included the Jackson County portion of the Kentucky Highlands EZ, the Mid-Delta EZ (Mississippi), the Rio Grande Valley EZ (Texas), the Accomack-Northampton EC (Virginia), the Central Savannah River Area EC (Georgia), the Greater Portsmouth EC (Ohio), the Greene-Sumter EC (Alabama), the McDowell County EC (West Virginia), the City of Watsonville EC (California), and the La Jicarita EC (New Mexico).

81

impact of community-development block grants (Parachini, 1997). More recent initiatives have focused on empowerment evaluation (Fetterman, Kaftarian, and Wandersman, 1996), and on approaches to evaluation of comprehensive community-development programs (Connell, Kubisch, Schorr, and Weiss, 1995).

This chapter focuses on the Learning Initiative, a project founded by the University of Tennessee's Community Partnership Center (CPC) to pilot participatory monitoring and evaluation in connection with the rural Empowerment Zones/Enterprise Communities (EZ/EC) program. Established by the Clinton Administration in 1993, the EZ/EC program is the most comprehensive program in recent years aimed at relieving severe distress in rural and urban areas. As part of the Learning Initiative, citizen learning teams worked with researchers in ten of the thirty-three EZ/EC sites during 1996–1997 to track the progress of the program toward selected goals, to document lessons learned for community development, and to make recommendations regarding improvement of the EZ/EC program at the local and federal levels. (For further background see Gaventa, Morrissey, and Edwards, 1995; Morrissey, Gaventa, and Creed, 1997; Community Partnership Center, 1998.) After first providing a brief description of the rural EZ/EC program and how the Learning Initiative evolved, this chapter will assess the approach that was used and the key lessons learned from this process.

## The Empowerment Zones/Enterprise Communities Program

Congress created the federal EZ/EC program in Title XIII of the Omnibus Budget Reconciliation Act of 1993, which President Bill Clinton signed into law on August 10, 1993. The bill authorized $2.5 billion in tax incentives and $1 billion in Title XX block grants to revitalize 104 distressed urban and rural communities. The White House created the Community Empowerment Board, an interagency task force led by Vice President Albert Gore, to oversee the program and related initiatives. The U.S. Department of Housing and Urban Development administers the urban part of the program, and the U.S. Department of Agriculture (USDA) administers the rural part.

The EZ/EC program is different from many federal programs in that it charges local communities with responsibility for developing their own strategic vision for change by focusing especially on economic opportunity, sustainable community development, and community-based partnerships. In each of these areas, community participation was to be critical. As the guidelines established by the President's Community Empowerment Board stated, "The road to economic opportunity and community development starts with broad participation by all segments of the community. [These] may include, among others, the political and governmental leadership, community groups, health and social service groups, environmental groups, religious organizations, the private and non-profit sectors, centers of learning and other community institutions. *The residents themselves, however, are the most important element of revitalization"* (U.S. Department of Agriculture, 1994, emphasis added).

More than five hundred communities entered the competitive process outlined by the federal guidelines and submitted their own strategic plans for community revitalization by June 30, 1994. In December 1994, three rural Empowerment Zones and thirty rural Enterprise Communities were designated (among others); each received significant block grants and other economic benefits.

## The Community Partnership Center Learning Initiative

As a community-development initiative, the EZ/EC program is significant partly because its guidelines articulated an approach that would enable people to develop solutions to rural poverty based on their own vision and participation. The program thus offered an important opportunity not only to learn lessons about participatory community development but also to pilot new approaches to evaluation of comprehensive community-revitalization initiatives that would be consistent with this philosophy.

Following the announcement of the program in early 1994, the CPC was approached by several urban and rural communities seeking assistance in the strategic-planning and application process. At a meeting in Washington, John Gaventa, one of the codirectors of the CPC, described the growing grassroots mobilization he saw as communities rushed to participate in the EZ/EC program. He asked an official in the USDA what steps were being taken to document and learn from the new program. Later, the official asked the CPC to submit a proposal to develop an approach to document and evaluate the rural part of the EZ/EC program and to do so in a way that would keep the program consistent with its participatory, bottom-up principles. The official later said, "We were much more interested in the difference the EZ/EC was making on the ground than we were in some kind of abstract, quantitative analysis. It you want the difference it's making on the ground, the best way to find that out is to involve people on the ground and give them a way of telling you that. We tried very intentionally to create a learning strategy that would tell us what was happening and would produce information that could improve what was happening at ground zero."

From the initial stages of the project, it was clear that an ongoing evaluation of this program would face a number of challenges. The thirty-three communities were scattered across poor parts of rural United States and were extremely diverse. Their goals for community revitalization, identified in the strategic-planning process, reflected this diversity. Moreover, many of the expressed goals were social and qualitative in nature—for example, empowerment, capacity building, participation, cultural pride; such goals are difficult to measure using traditional economic-development indicators. In the early days of the program, the designated communities were required by Washington to develop and negotiate measurable benchmarks in order to receive funding. This requirement quickly became a source of frustration and disempowerment, as communities and even the technical staff working with them often lacked the experience and know-how necessary to develop indicators for tracking progress toward intangible outcomes.

## The Need for a Participatory Approach

In the first year of the project, the CPC team and regionally based researchers visited most of the designated communities to gather baseline information and to develop an appropriate evaluation plan. Usually, in such programs, evaluation is done by outside experts and is based on externally developed indicators of progress. The initial field work pointed to the need to develop a new approach, one which would recognize the diverse contexts and goals of the participating communities, the intangible and nonquantifiable nature of many of the goals, and the difficulties of using standardized, traditional indicators to track a program rooted in local planning and promises of flexibility in meeting local needs (*The Evaluation and Learning Initiative . . .*, 1995).

In addition, the first phase of the work pointed to the need to strengthen and promote citizen participation and capacity building in the program monitoring and assessment process itself. And because a goal of the EZ/EC program was to enable communities to develop their own strategic vision and capacity for change, it was important that communities learn how to work together to monitor and measure their own progress. In order to fully realize the continuous learning and improvement emphasized in the program, there was a need for a systematic, community-driven process for local documentation and learning. To be consistent with the participatory process on which development plans had been built, local people also needed to be involved in creating their own indicators of progress and approaches for evaluating them (*Feuerstein,* 1986).

## The Structure and Process of the Learning Initiative

With these needs in mind, and with the financial support and collaboration of USDA and the Ford Foundation, in early 1996 the CPC Learning Initiative began to pilot a participatory evaluation (PE) approach in ten rural EZ/EC sites. In each site, citizen learning teams, led by a local coordinator, were formed to monitor early implementation of the program and to begin to track progress toward key goals. Each learning team consisted of five to twenty-five local people who represented a cross-section of community stakeholders including local residents and members of the local EZ/EC board and other community organizations. Regional researchers helped to facilitate the process and to report the results and lessons to the University of Tennessee. The CPC in turn coordinated the process and compiled and reported the findings to the project sponsors and other interested parties.

Most of the ten citizen learning teams were located in the historically poorest rural regions of the United States, including the coastal and delta South, the Appalachian region, and the southwestern border states.

Over a period of approximately twelve months, each learning team followed a ten-month process known as the Learning Wheel (see Figure 6.1). These are the main activities of the Learning Wheel:

- Defining indicators of success for one or more goals
- Measuring and monitoring to document results
- Analyzing the results
- Deciding how to take action for continuous improvement

**Figure 6.1. The Learning Wheel**

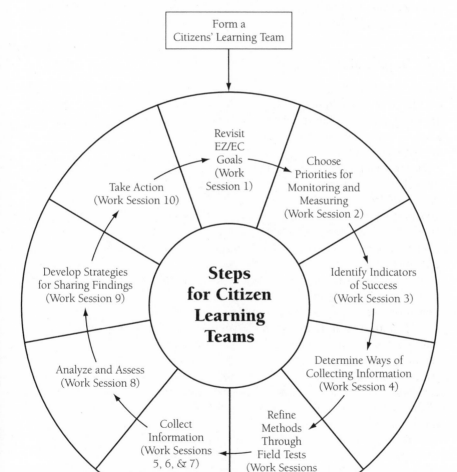

The learning teams undertook each major activity of the Learning Wheel with the support of the regional researchers, who facilitated the process, documented results, and provided research skills. In addition, the Learning Initiative provided training and capacity-building activities for local coordinators, learning teams, and regional researchers. Hosted by local EZ/EC communities, these workshops allowed the opportunity for training in the model, sharing lessons, cross-site mentoring and exchange, and building new skills. In addition, each local coordinator and researcher received training materials, including a trainers' manual, a workbook for team members, and a packet of resource materials on participatory monitoring and evaluation, popular research methods, and community-based indicators. Each learning team also received a small grant of $10,000 to help support their activities; these grants were used primarily to provide a stipend to the local coordinator, though much of the work was carried out by volunteers.

## The Impact of the Process

From the beginning, the CPC recognized that the project would be experimental, that it would not provide a comprehensive evaluation of all aspects of the program, and that it would involve methods and results different from those of conventional, external evaluation studies (Narayan-Parker, 1993). Participatory monitoring and evaluation involves the program beneficiaries in deciding which goals are most important and in assessing how well these goals are achieved. In the process, it tries to build the knowledge and capacity of communities to do their own evaluations and to use the lessons learned in the process to improve the implementation of the program at the local and national level. The effectiveness of the approach used can be assessed by examining the contribution of the process to research and evaluation, especially through local documentation and learning; to capacity building, through development of the skills and leadership of local participants in rural EZ/EC communities; and to continuous improvement of the program, through strengthened citizen participation, feedback, and accountability.

**Research and Evaluation.** Participatory monitoring and evaluation emphasizes the importance of having citizens learn to carry out their own research to assess the performance of local development efforts. A clear contribution of the Learning Initiative was seen in the involvement of local citizens and regional researchers in providing documentation on and assessment of the EZ/EC program. The research itself was a significant accomplishment for many of the teams.

Teams from the ten participating communities submitted a case study of their process and findings by mid-1977 (Community Partnership Center, 1998). Throughout the process, dozens of local volunteers spent many hours selecting goals and indicators, deciding on tools and sources of data, gathering new information, developing lessons and findings, and communicating them to local, state, and national decision-making bodies.

Many team members found that the Learning Wheel was a more complex, interactive process than they had expected, and they made adjustments to fit their own situations. For example, most learning teams realized early on that, in order to make the monitoring and measuring process manageable, they had to narrow the research focus. The Learning Initiative staff and consultants guided several learning teams to focus on just one goal. Other teams used multiple goals and indicators.

The various data-gathering tools that teams developed or used in the field (or both) cover an extremely wide range. They included interviews, focus groups, reviews of public documents, content analyses, media analyses, questionnaires, mapping, personal observations, use rates for facilities and services, windshield surveys, oral histories, educational test scores, and informal communications.

In one particularly innovative effort, in McDowell County, West Virginia, the team wanted to develop baseline data for determining whether the presence of social capital affects community revitalization, including communities' ability to access critical resources. The team undertook a mapping project of the numbers and types of community organizations in each of the seventy-eight communities of the county. The types included those initiated from within the community and those imported into the community or controlled by elite bodies. Working from telephone directories, service directories, and local knowledge, the team developed a list of all organizations in each community. With this information, they developed indicators for those organizations that contributed to capacity building and those that did not, and they mapped the relationship of the capacity-building groups to the distribution of funds in the county. Among other results, the findings led to new insights about the level of organization and capacity building that already existed in the county.

**Capacity Building.** One important goal of the Learning Initiative itself was to strengthen the capacity of residents in the EZ/EC communities to participate in the monitoring and evaluation process as well as in broader aspects of community development. This goal is an essential aspect of an empowerment program. Moreover, field work during the first year of the rural EZ/EC evaluation project had pointed to local capacity building as a major need.

At the Texas cross-site workshop, participants analyzed how the Learning Initiative contributed to personal growth, interpreted broadly to mean capacity or leadership development. Team members felt that they gained credibility and visibility in their communities through the process and that they had acquired new skills and knowledge of how to do research.

Overall, the learning-team model encourages and supports people who would not otherwise be involved in the community's development. The learning-team model "authorizes" citizens to participate in decision making in their community. Team members learn how their community works and share this knowledge with others. As they gather data, they are also engaged in community education and in providing an avenue for participation. Each team had members who grew in confidence and skill and who became involved in other public roles in the community.

A critical part of the capacity-building process was the training workshops, which brought local project leaders together in different locations on three occasions: at the beginning, midway through, and toward the end of the process. As one person described her own growth in self-confidence, "In Boggs, Georgia, it was 'Oh Lord, I don't know what I am going to do with this.' In New Mexico, it was like, 'Yeah we can do this.' And here we are in Texas, and we've done it!"

**Continuous Improvement.** Through the strengthened capacity and involvement of local citizens, as well as through sharing research findings, the Learning Initiative project also hoped to contribute to ongoing improvement of the EZ/EC program as well as to provide an accountability mechanism for keeping residents informed about EZ/EC activities and progress.

For instance, in Jackson County, Kentucky, the learning-team coordinator attended almost five hundred meetings in one year (averaging about twenty-five a week), monitoring decisions that were being made in board, project, subcommittee, and local government meetings. She stated, "In order to know my empowerment Zone, you had to know your city government and how everything works." In carrying out such ongoing monitoring, members of the learning team viewed themselves as playing an important role as watchdogs, working to make the process conform to the original guidelines of the program.

However, when the Kentucky team's report became public, it led to a great deal of controversy. While pointing to a number of positive accomplishments of the program in the community, the report also raised a number of questions, especially about the limited citizen participation in the implementation of various projects. A spokesperson for the county's established leadership responded by labeling the report "not only ignorant but completely stupid." Meanwhile one of the leading newspapers in the state took the learning team's side, writing, "Count us among the stupid, because the report rings true" ("Ill at Ease with EZ," 1997). At the same time, the local EZ/EC agency wrote to Washington criticizing the learning for "serious flaws in the research process" and for not including a "statistically significant or random" sample. But an experienced community-development worker in the area wrote that the "Kentucky community evaluation team has created quite a stir with its report, in which they spoke truth to power."

In time, the controversy helped to create an environment for positive reform. Because of the learning team's efforts to document the EZ/EC process and the barriers to participation, along with the willingness of several board members to engage citizens in dialogue about their findings, several important policy changes were initiated to strengthen community participation and to reorganize several of the community projects.

In other communities, the relationship between the learning teams and the local Empowerment Zones was less acrimonious. Some teams functioned more as inside learning groups rather than as external watchdogs, with members primarily people already involved in project implementation. In a third model, perhaps the most effective, there was openness and support for the learning-team process from project leaders, but the teams had enough autonomy to pursue their evaluation independently and then feed back the findings. This model required having local project or political leaders who were open to external inquiry. As one such leader said, "The EC board and staff want to support the learning team and learn from it. If the evaluation puts a negative light on what [the project] is doing, we want to know that and improve on it."

## Impact on the National Level

One important innovation of the project was the use of "EZ/EC roundtable seminars," in which representatives from the learning teams came to Washington to share their findings with officials in the USDA, the President's Community Empowerment Board, and others involved in the EZ/EC program. Although it is hard to assess the impact of these sessions on the program leaders, they did provide an important feedback loop from the grassroots teams to Washington. For the teams, these sessions strengthened their credibility locally. The fact that they were going to Washington to report their findings attracted the attention of local officials accustomed to being the sole channel of communication to program funders and federal officials.

At the same time, throughout the project, there were enormous challenges in matching the participatory approach to the culture and requirements of a complicated federal agency and national program. For various technical reasons, the project had been supported from one Under Secretary's office, though money came through another Under Secretary's office to monitor and evaluate a program administered by yet a third office. Although the Policy and Planning Office had agreed to, and had supported, the participatory approach, other officials within the agency did not support it or, for that matter, understand it. Those responsible for program implementation seemed interested in a traditional evaluation design, which could help them demonstrate progress to Congress and to the White House, especially as such an approach would measure tangible outputs, such as jobs and infrastructure.

The division over what the evaluation ought to look like was compounded by other factors inherent in working with a government agency. Continuous staff turnover of political appointees, including the departure of the original, high-level champion within the agency, meant that understanding of, knowledge of, and expectations for the project were constantly changing. Competition and conflict between departments aggravated disagreements over the direction of the evaluation. The high political profile of the EZ/EC program also meant that lower political appointees and agency staff were concerned about how criticisms of the project would be received. Although to some within the USDA and the White House the evaluation project represented the grassroots empowerment and participation the program was supposed to be about, others believed the participatory methodology could not be used to defend the programs effectively and to gain additional funding from Congress.

These divisions had serious consequences for the effectiveness of the project. The lack of consistent, visible support for the project at a high level meant that the CPC project staff were constantly mediating the conflicting expectations of various players within the federal agency, as well as state and local officials. The ambivalence (and, in some cases, hostility) in the agency in turn filtered down to the EZ/EC communities, where local officials could cite the lack of full support as a reason to ignore or discredit the local teams. (After one meeting, EZ/EC staff interpreted statements from a Washington official to mean that they no longer should participate in the process, and they stopped attending learning-team meetings.) The conflicts and competing demands also meant that the central CPC staff found themselves constantly defending the process or responding to rumors, such as that funds for the project were to be withdrawn or redirected. These activities drew valuable time and resources away from supporting the learning teams.

By the third year, these conflicts were taking their toll. On the one hand, we had learned a great deal and had developed an approach for citizen monitoring and evaluation that could be shared with others. On the other hand, the leaders of the project felt that the process lacked the clear political support it needed in Washington to be effective. After completing the final reports from the pilot process, we chose not to continue the project in connection with the EZ/EC program. At the same time, the Ford Foundation provided funds to continue independently. In March 1998, for instance, the Learning Initiative sponsored a national workshop at which participants from across the country learned about the approach and how it could be adapted in other community-development efforts.

## Lessons and Implications

It is perhaps too early to tell what the overall impact of the Learning Initiative will be or to draw final conclusions about the use of participatory approaches in the monitoring and evaluation of public programs. Nevertheless, several key themes emerge.

**Citizen Participation.** Often in participatory development, participation may be strong in the planning phase of a program but decline in later stages. The learning teams have shown potential as a vehicle for sustaining citizen participation in public programs beyond the planning stages and for improving them as a result. Informed citizens can actively and effectively hold their leaders and institutions accountable and can share information with others. In this regard, the learning teams contributed to the program's broad goals of strengthening partnership and local empowerment. And learning teams have demonstrated that their research can stimulate discussion about community change and improvement.

**Deciding What to Measure.** Changing who is involved in the evaluation process can change what is measured and can alter priorities. For instance, despite the importance of such concepts as participation, partnership, and collaboration in the published guidelines and in public talk about the EZ/EC program, those responsible for implementation of the program in Washington did not include a requirement to report progress on these goals. Rather, the traditional and tangible goals of economic and infrastructure development were emphasized. Participation was seen more as a means to meet these goals than as an important program outcome in and of itself. To the learning teams, however, citizen participation was one of the most important program goals to be tracked.

**Deciding Who Participates.** Not only does participation in the evaluation change the priorities, but it also raises the equally contentious question of who should participate. Which stakeholders should be involved? For the CPC project leaders and for the learning teams, it was important that the beneficiaries, the local residents, lead the evaluation process at the local level. To some in Washington, the stakeholders also included state and local officials, other agencies, or their own staff—a much broader and potentially more powerful set of actors than the local residents. Here the differences between beneficiary participation and stakeholder participation, and the challenges of combining the two, became clear. Although in some ideal sense the PE process can involve negotiation and involvement by all levels, in reality such involvement is difficult because of preexisting distrust or conflict. In some communities, involving local citizens in a process that they could consider their own meant excluding other stakeholders who were seen as always being in charge or not to be trusted. However, once these other stakeholders were excluded, or not actively included, it became difficult to gain their support for the process. The degree to which beneficiaries or stakeholders from differing groups and agencies can be involved depends very much on their history of working together—that is, on the levels of social capital that already exist and that can be drawn on to support such a process (Putnam, 1993).

**Methodological Conflict and Methodological Learning.** Who the participants are in an evaluation process will affect what the most important objectives will be; conversely, the purposes of the evaluation will affect the levels and types of participation that are most important. In this project, the most important outcomes for local participants were learning and capacity building, as well as gaining information and skills that could be used immediately to improve program implementation in the community. For at least some of the Washington stakeholders, the most important objective was obtaining standardized, outcome-oriented data, which they could use to provide evidence of their accountability to Congress or their superiors and could increase the program's political capital or be used to obtain additional program funds.

The tension over which objective was most important was often played out in conflicts over appropriate methodology. For instance, to the learning teams, one of the most important parts of the process was the opportunity to come together with those from other communities to exchange findings and experiences and to build networks for future learning and action through the cross-site workshops. To one of the officials in Washington, this process did not square with a traditional evaluation process, in which outside researchers would study the communities and then compare results. In his view, allowing the participants to meet and share learning "contaminated" the results. Similarly, findings of the learning teams were attacked as mere "perceptions," whereas, from another point of view, the discovery of "meaning" by key stakeholders is a critical part of a qualitative and participatory process. Differences also emerged over the appropriate role of the researchers—were they to serve as facilitators of a learning process or as outside, "objective" observers; over the issue of standardized versus contextual indicators; even over whether the work of the learning teams should be called program evaluation or something else.

Underlying all these debates were not only critical differences in objectives but also a lack of acceptance or awareness by government officials about the methods and validity of the qualitative and participatory approaches that are now widely used in the evaluation field. While international-development agencies such as the World Bank or the United Nations Development Program have developed manuals for staff on the new "learning-process" approaches of development (as opposed to "blueprint" approaches) and on related participatory processes of evaluation (United Nations Development Program, 1997), agencies concerned with community development within the United States have not done so. For instance, at the same time that officials at USDA were questioning the participatory evaluation methodology, the U.S. Agency for International Development invited representatives of the citizen learning teams to speak to its staff, asked the CPC to host a Lessons Without Borders conference, and published a report on PE for its international staff. This lack of awareness and sensitivity to participatory methods on the part of agency staff points to the need for training and capacity building at the government and technical level, as well as at the community level, and to the need for domestic and international programs to learn from one another. Similarly, project leaders, who had experience working with participatory approaches at the community level, had less experience in working with government agencies and also could have benefitted from learning from others about doing so.

**Evaluation as a Social and Political Process.** Ultimately it became clear that PE is as much a social and political process as it is a research process. As such, new skills and methods are needed, ones that trained researchers and evaluators may not already have. The need for team building, negotiation, conflict resolution, stakeholder involvement, facilitation, and group leadership skills was seen at almost every step and level of the process, within the learning teams as well as between the teams and other players.

An important contribution of the project was the way in which this learning about the social and group nature of PE was applied toward improvement of the Learning Wheel itself. Toward the end of the pilot process, a group of learning-team members, researchers, and staff met to reflect on the process. They revised the wheel, adding several important steps overlooked by the researcher-planners in the first approach. One addition created a step at the beginning on building a team, including how to recognize and affirm diversity and how to make decisions and reach consensus. Another addition was a step for "applying the learning cycle to ourselves and our work"—that is, using the process in a recursive way to ensure that the group is always measuring its own work and process against its goals. The group added "celebrating victories" and "recognizing and honoring the role and contribution of team members, staff, and others"—a critical part of team and community building. Finally, the group added a step entitled "what next"—reflecting on the process and planning and acting to sustain it.

**Sustainability of the Process.**  In order to be sustainable, such a process requires long-term commitment and a sensitivity on the part of funders and technical-assistance providers to the time required by community groups to build working teams, gather information, develop consensus, and take action. In this case, almost all the learning teams felt they needed more time and support for the process to unfold. Volunteers put in considerable time, and the stipends provided to local coordinators were unrealistically low given the expectations of them. At the same time, Washington was eager to see results and to get information that could be used as soon as possible. Equally problematic was the driving force of the government's fiscal year. Decisions about funding were always made late in the fiscal year, and only with one-year commitments, creating enormous uncertainty in all participants about whether they could give a long-term commitment to the project. One interesting indicator of sustainability of the project, however, proved to be the ways in which team members used the model and adapted it to other projects or initiatives in their community. For instance, in one community a local learning-team coordinator applied the model to state welfare reform; in another, students formed a learning team to evaluate the performance of their high school.

**Scaling Up and Institutional Change.**  Ultimately, no matter how good the process, to engage the beneficiaries of development in judging what works and what does not, what constitutes success and what does not, is to open up much broader questions of whose values are important, of what we want our communities and societies to be and to become. Facing these questions will inevitably involve conflicts of perspective and of interest and may threaten the status quo.

PE offers one proactive way to create processes in which these important questions can emerge and to address them through a structured learning process. Although the potential of PE has been proven at the micro level, the challenge now is how to scale up the processes and to apply them to and incorporate them within large programs and institutions. To do so requires effective champions in the institutions themselves, leaders who have the capacity and commitment to take the risks of creating a space for creative questioning, learning, and conflict. It also requires certain levels of social capital or at least a commitment by groups to work together despite differences. It requires creating and supporting within communities and organizations new cultures and environments where learning both for program accountability and for broad community and institutional change can occur. The experience of the Learning Initiative shows that these are enormous challenges, but challenges well worth pursuing in the coming decade.

## References

Community Partnership Center. *Findings and Recommendations of the Community Partnership Center EZ/EC Learning Initiative.* Knoxville: Community Partnership Center, University of Tennessee, 1998.

Connell, J. P., Kubisch, A. C., Schorr, L. B., and Weiss, C. H. (eds.). *New Approaches to Evaluating Community Initiatives: Concepts, Methods, and Contexts.* Washington, D.C.: Roundtable on Comprehensive Community Initiatives for Children and Families, Aspen Institute, 1995.

Estrella, M., and Gaventa, J. "Who Counts Reality?" In *Participatory Monitoring and Evaluation: A Literature Review.* Working Paper. Sussex, England: Institute for Development Studies, 1998.

*The Evaluation and Learning Initiative of the National Empowerment Zone and Enterprise Community Program: Review and Recommendations for Phase II Support.* Vol. 1: *Project Overview and Recommendations;* Vol. 2: *Literature Review.* Knoxville: Community Partnership Center, University of Tennessee, 1995.

Fetterman, D. M., Kaftarian, S. J., and Wandersman, A. *Empowerment Evaluation: Knowledge and Tools for Self-Assessment and Accountability.* Thousand Oaks, Calif.: Sage, 1996.

Feuerstein, M.-T. *Partners in Evaluation: Evaluating Development and Community Programmes with Participants.* London: Macmillan, 1986.

Gaventa, J., Morrissey, J., and Edwards, W. R. "Empowering People: Goals and Realities." *Forum for Applied Research and Public Policy,* 1995, *10* (4), 116–121.

"Ill at Ease with EZ." *Lexington Herald Leader,* Feb. 8 and 11, 1997.

Morrissey, J., Gaventa, J., and Creed, V. *Preliminary Findings from Phase I of the Rural EZ/EC Evaluation Project.* Knoxville: Community Partnership Center, University of Tennessee, 1997.

Narayan-Parker, D. *Participatory Evaluation: Tools for Managing Change in Water and Sanitation.* World Bank Technical Paper 207. Washington, D.C.: World Bank, 1993.

Parachini, L., with Mott, A. "Strengthening Community Voices in Policy Reform." In *Community-Based Monitoring, Learning and Action Strategies for an Era of Development and Change.* Washington, D.C.: Center for Community Change, 1997.

Putnam, R. D. "The Prosperous Community: Social Capital and Public Life." *American Prospect,* 1993, *13,* 35–42.

United Nations Development Program. *Who Are the Question Makers? A Participatory Evaluation Handbook.* New York: Office of Evaluation and Strategic Planning, United Nations Development Program, 1997.

U.S. Department of Agriculture. *Building Communities Together. Rural Guidebook for Strategic Planning.* Washington, D.C.: U.S. Department of Agriculture, 1994.

*JOHN GAVENTA, fellow at the Institute of Development Studies, University of Sussex, was the founder and initial director of the Learning Initiative.*

*VICTORIA CREED followed John Gaventa as the director of the Learning Initiative; she also has her own consultant practice, Learning Partners, in Knoxville, Tennessee.*

*JANICE MORRISSEY was research coordinator of the Learning Initiative and now is a consultant with Assessment & Monitoring Alternatives, Kingston, Tennessee.*

*Reflections on theory from practice are addressed.*


# Final Commentary

*Elizabeth Whitmore*


What have we learned about participatory evaluation (PE)? How do the practice examples respond to the conceptual challenges posed in the first three chapters of this volume?

Let's examine three questions: (1) To what extent are the three dimensions of participation offered in Chapter One—depth of participation, range of stakeholders involved, and control of the process by evaluators and stakeholders—present in practice? How do the case examples inform our understanding of these dimensions and their interconnections? (2) Given their historical roots, are practical participatory evaluation (P-PE) and transformative participatory evaluation (T-PE) different in important ways in practice? What new dimensions of difference, or commonality, are revealed by the cases? (3) What have we learned from the case examples about the principles, processes, and "key moments" of PE implementation?


## The Three Dimensions of Participation

It is not too difficult to "locate" each case study somewhere on each of the three dimensions. None used "consultation" but rather engaged participants in some depth in the process. All involved a fairly broad range of participants, which worked better in some instances (for King, once the managers were included) than others (Gaventa, Creed, and Morrissey refer to the problems of inclusion and exclusion in the citizen learning teams). In all three cases, practitioners or community people had considerable control of the process.

Clearly, these dimensions interconnect. The more depth of participation, the more likely participants are to control the process. The greater the range of participants, the more complex the issues of control. A broad range of participants does not exclude deep participation (as in King), but they may need to work separately, as the Chapter Six authors conclude in their discussion of the gap between community groups and government officials. One can consult with a broad range of stakeholders; indeed this is a common approach. Clearly, in this case, control remains in the hands of the evaluator. Perhaps "consultation" and "evaluator control" should not be included in a participatory framework at all because, at best, they imply rather token participation.

To varying degrees, evaluators in the case examples struggled with the issues implicit in the three dimensions. A major one, raised in all the chapters, is power and control. Power differences become a serious complication, internally and externally. If key stakeholders do not cooperate, they can (and do) block the process. In all three instances, this was a problem. All case evaluators conclude that there is a need for consistent and visible support of the project at high levels. So, how, then, do we "hand over the stick"—that is, give control to participants? In fact, control seems to have been handed over successfully at the participant level in all three cases. The problem, then, is political, as Gaventa, Creed, and Morrissey conclude. Evaluators have struggled with the politics of evaluation for a long time. In PE the macropolitics of power and resource control are further compounded by micropolitical contestations over power and the control of resources.

There are limitations in practitioner-controlled evaluations, as there are in researcher-controlled ones. If stakeholders have complete control, there is a risk of "uneven" results (Chapter Five); if they have no control, stakeholders lose interest and feel no sense of responsibility or accountability for what happens (King). The authors of Chapter Six note that participants lacked the expertise to develop "measurable benchmarks," and this led to frustration by everyone involved. It is absurd to expect untrained people to conduct complicated statistical studies. But there are many other methods of gathering information that people can learn and understand and that can produce results of high quality. Perhaps the problem is how "measurable benchmarks" or "outcomes" get defined, by whom, and for what purpose. The pitfalls of researcher-controlled evaluations are well known (stakeholder alienation, lack of evaluation experience in or familiarity with a community, mistrust of outsiders, assumptions about how the world works, standpoint based on gender, class, or race). In the end, no one "extreme" is likely to work well. But the combination, creatively crafted in a given situation, offers the opportunity for getting it right. These case studies seem to confirm this assumption.

## Differences Between P-PE and T-PE in Practice

When we examine what the evaluators actually did in the case examples, there are more similarities than differences. All three spent considerable time and effort building trust with and among participants. All worked hard, in a facilitation role, to help participants acquire the knowledge and skills necessary to conduct an evaluation. All recognized the importance of building and supporting leadership. Outside facilitators were key in all three studies. They all had to struggle with complex interpersonal and group dynamics and with the political realities of power and control. All produced high-quality data.

There are some differences, at least in emphasis. The differing roots of P-PE and T-PE practitioners do shape their focus—one on use, the other more on empowerment, primarily through capacity building. T-PE practitioners are more likely to build control by stakeholders into their design. They focus intentionally on those with less power in a situation, while P-PE practitioners work mainly with primary users. The techniques also vary. T-PE evaluators are using a broad range of tools devised in international development (notably the Participatory Rural Appraisal tools developed by R. Chambers and others), which P-PE people might want to investigate.

King's comment that the three E's (empowerment, enlightenment, and emancipation) cannot be assumed necessarily to follow from her efforts is an important caution for all PE evaluators. A number of critiques in the T-PE field raise similar issues. There is a danger in PE, especially T-PE given its ideological base, of being "on a mission," of being overzealous in efforts to "transform" society. The PE evaluator needs to be systematically reflective and build in ways to counteract any very human attempts to manipulate or subtly direct the process. In the Haiti example, the funders had specifically set up a participatory process. The trainers first spent time "initiating participants into the world of PE"; not surprisingly, the participants "chose" PE in the subsequent exercise. The evaluator does influence the process; that is clear. The challenge is to remain, in practice, true to the underlying principles.

King concludes, quite eloquently, that there is one important dimension missing, one that captures her "ongoing and primary commitment to improving social institutions." P-PE's emphasis on use may assume this commitment but does not state it up front in the same way that T-PE does. This difference offers food for thought in terms of how one might expand or revise the PE framework.

## The Principles, Processes, and "Key Moments" of PE Implementation

All three examples demonstrate the principles and processes outlined in Chapter Three. They vary, of course, in how these are achieved because the case contexts vary. Each case does highlight certain issues, however, and offers us some insight into which practices worked well and which did not. They all tell us that PE is a complex, time-consuming, and risky business. They also tell us that working with people in this way can be exhilarating and that it can produce high-quality outcomes, both technical as well as human.

There appear to be five essential ingredients in making PE work. First, a generally *receptive context* is key. Not surprisingly, PE works best when everyone (from top to bottom) is on board and when the organizational climate is fairly open and democratic. Attempting PE in top-down, hierarchical settings produces headaches for both the evaluator and the participants and may well end up making things worse by promising what it cannot deliver.

Second, the evaluator's *commitment* to participation and faith in the inherent capacity of people to contribute meaningfully to the evaluation process are critical ingredients. They allow the evaluator to be comfortable with sharing power and control, to really "hand over the stick." Without these fundamental beliefs, an evaluator may incorporate PE because it seems trendy or because one "ought" to do it, but such an approach is bound to fail.

Third, PE takes *time;* it cannot be rushed. We can condense human learning and the change process just so much. The problem is that we operate in a system that tends to demand "measurable results" in the short term. Even administrators committed to participatory approaches find themselves having to convince superiors to hold off and allow the process to work.

Fourth, *"people skills,"* particularly facilitation, are a key part of a participatory evaluator's toolkit. The collaborative effort, in whatever form, requires particular attitudes and skills. The role of the evaluator is thus changed dramatically from that of technical expert only. We need training in the science and art of negotiation, team building, conflict resolution, involving stakeholders, reflexivity. PE puts the burden on the evaluator to be skilled in working cooperatively, in being willing and able to share experiences, knowledge, insights, and, perhaps most difficult, power. Working with people is messy, unpredictable, often frustrating, complicated. Yet I would argue that it is the only way, in the end, that we can really succeed in "getting it right." Evaluation as a social and political process is reinforced in this volume. It means, as most of the authors have demonstrated, that we need to be comfortable with much more ambiguity than our traditional social science training has prepared us for.

Fifth, each case study also successfully engaged stakeholders in the process and achieved the objective of *capacity building.* The question one might ask is why do an evaluation if the real objective is learning and strengthening skills? Isn't our goal to improve programs or to measure impact? Participatory evaluators argue that capacity building is an essential component of evaluation for three reasons. (1) Capacity building is *consistent with the goals* of most social and educational programs and with the values and principles of democracy.

(2) Capacity building enhances *accountability.* The collective process is one way to keep people honest. Informed, involved, and knowledgeable stakeholders are likely to know about their program and their community and to ask questions of each other and of those in positions of responsibility. Coupal and Simoneau struggled with the negative attitudes of the facilitators toward the people they were supposed to be serving. The participatory process clearly helped them examine those attitudes and become more accountable to their constituents. Gaventa, Creed, and Morrissey found that participants were extremely diligent in monitoring decisions and got to know how their local governments worked. Learning-team members came to view themselves "as playing an important role as watchdogs, working to make the process conform to the original guidelines of the program."

(3) Capacity building further supports *sustainability* through leadership development, building a core of participants who are committed to the program and knowledgeable about it. The process energizes people, keeps them going. In King's examples, participants assumed ownership of the data, and the

result was increased use and commitment. In the Haitian evaluation, the facilitators changed their views on how development should happen; they took ownership, in a personal and professional sense, of the process. The network they formed afterward further supports this conclusion. The data produced resulted directly from their own work with people in their communities and have formed a basis for future planning. As a result, the facilitators are committed to seeing the process work.

In the end, PE offers us an opportunity. Two authors in this volume sum it up well. King concludes, "I am not concerned with labels; what matters to me is the increasing ability of our field to learn from these approaches and to use them appropriately and effectively." And Gaventa, Creed, and Morrissey state, "No matter how good the process, to engage the beneficiaries of development in judging what works and what does not, what constitutes success and what does not, is to open up much broader questions of whose values are important, of what we want our communities and societies to be and to become. Facing these questions will inevitably involve conflicts of perspective and of interest and may threaten the status quo. PE offers one proactive way to create processes in which these important questions can emerge and to address them through a structured learning process."

# INDEX

Action Research Facilitation (ARF) Committee, 59–60
Addams, J., 58
Adorno, T. W., 8
Alinsky, S., 30
Alvik, T., 12
Argyris, C., 13
Aristide, J.-B., 69
Ayers, T. D., 7

Benhabib, S., 32
Bias debate, 34
Bloom, G. A., 10, 15
Brunner, I., 9
Bryk, A. S., 12
Bush Educators' Program (BEP) [Paine case study], 62

Campbell, D. T., 27
Canada-Haiti Humanitarian Alliance Fund, 70, 77–78. *See also* Haitian participatory evaluation (PE)
Canadian Council for International Cooperation (CCIC), 70
Canadian Development Agency, 33
Canadian International Development Agency, 70
Capacity building: in EZ/EC communities, 87–88; objective of achieving, 46, 76, 98–99
Carr, W., 13
Center for Community Change, 81–82
Chambers, R., 35, 36
Chelimsky, E., 27
Citizens' Learning Team, 85–86
Collaborative action research: defining, 59; Minneapolis Community Services (MCS) Project case study of, 59–60; as participatory model, 33; practical guidelines for, 62–65; Thomas Paine Professional Practice School case study of, 60–62
Collaborative evaluation: overview of specific forms of, 12–13; PE approach compared to, 14–16
Communication, 63
Community Partnership Center (CPC), 82
Community Partnership Center Learning

Initiative: establishment of, 82, 83–84; structure and process f, 84–86. *See also* Empowerment Zones/Enterprise Communities (EZ/EC) program
Control of the evaluation process, 10, 11
Cooperative inquiry: described, 17; systematic inquiry by goals/process dimensions of, 13
Cousins, J. B., 6, 10, 11, 12, 14, 15, 23, 25, 59, 65
Cracknell, B., 35
Creed, V., 94, 96, 99
Critical theory, 31–32, 33
Cross-cultural issues, 18
Cuevara, C., 30
Cultural issues, 52

Data: decision making on collecting, 51–53; gathered on EZ/EC program, 86–87; Haitian PE interpretation and presentation of, 76–77; PE methodology and, 46; synthesizing, analyzing/verifying the, 53–54
Decision making: on data collection, 51–53; during methodology process, 47–48; evaluation approaches and, 28; key stakeholders involved in, 45; P-PE impact on, 6; P-PE support of, 6, 28; regarding methodology model, 46–47; T-PE on ethical, 33
Democratic evaluation: decision making and, 28; systematic inquiry by goals/process dimensions of, 12
Dependency theory, 8
Depth of participation, 10, 11
Developmental evaluation, 13
Dewey, J., 27, 58, 59
Diana, Princess, 66
Donohue, J. J., 10, 15

Earl, L. M., 7, 11, 12, 14, 59
Emancipation, 97
Emancipatory (participatory) action research, 13, 17
Empowerment: critical theory on, 31–32; as one of the three E's, 97; PE debate over, 36–37; T-PE promotion of, 44

Learning Wheel, 85–86, 87, 92
Legitimate knowledge, 44
Lessons Without Borders conference, 92
Levin, B., 10
Lewin, K., 27, 35

MacDonald, B., 12
McDowell County EZ/EC team, 87
McTaggart, R., 12, 13, 17
Mapping exercises, 74
Mark, M. M., 12, 15
Marx, K., 8, 30, 33
Minneapolis Community Services (MCS) Project case study, 59–60
Morrissey, J., 94, 96, 99

Nevo, D., 12, 16
Northern PE, 34–35
Nunneley, D., 59

Objectivity debate, 34
Omnibus Budget Reconciliation Act of 1993, 82
Organic intellectual concept, 31
Organizational power structure, 63–64
Organizational trust, 63
Orton, R., 59
Outcomes Accreditation (OA) Process (Paine case study), 61–62
Outside evaluators, 49
Outside facilitation, 65, 96

Papineau, D., 40
Participants: communication among, 63; in EZ/EC program citizen, 90–91; leadership among, 64; selection of, 18; trained in Haitian PE, 73–74; training of, 18–19. See also Evaluators;Facilitators
Participatory action research (PAR): development of, 16–17, 30; EZ/EC program, 86–87; systematic inquiry by goals/process dimensions of, 13
Participatory evaluation (PE): adopting standard methodology for, 52–53; assumptions of, 25; bad experience with, 57–59; compared to other collaborative evaluation forms, 14–16; conditions enabling, 19; controlling/using outcomes and reports on, 54–55; current issues/debates on, 33–37; defining, 59; developing action

plans for future through, 54; educational nature of, 46; evaluator role debate in, 37; guidelines for successful, 62–65; implementation of principles, processes, key moments of, 97–99; literature on, 9; Northern vs. Southern, 34–35; objectivity and bias debate in, 34; political nature of, 45–46; scaling up/institutional change through, 93–94; as social and political process, 92–93; stakeholder model and, 7; stakeholders and, 5–6; sustainability of process, 93; systematic inquiry by goals/process dimensions, 12; technical quality debate on, 36; three dimensions of, 10–11, 95–96; used in ten rural EZ/EC sites, 84–86; usefulness/utilization debate on, 35. See also Evaluation
Participatory evaluation (PE) methodology: adapting standard methods for, 52–53; assembling team for, 48–50; decisions made for, 47–48; developing plan for, 50–51; implementing process of, 46–55; key process elements of, 45–46; principles governing, 43–45; setting agenda for, 50–51
Participatory Learning and Action (PLA), 32, 73
Participatory models, 33
Participatory Research Group (Toronto), 8
Participatory Research Network, 29, 32
Participatory rural appraisal (PRA), 32–33, 73
Patton, M. Q., 13, 16, 28, 65
Peirce, C., 27
People skills, 98
Personal factor, 28
Philosophical antecedents: of P-PE, 27; of T-PE, 30–32
Positivist models, 8
Power: addressing inequities of stakeholders, 45; emancipatory social change and manipulation of, 31; evaluation and, 18; PE debate over, 36–37; shared between evaluator and stakeholders, 44; theoretical thinking on, 33
Power structure issues, 63–64
Practical participatory evaluation (P-PE): decision making and, 6, 28; defining, 6; development of, 6–7, 28–29; differences between T-PE and, 9–10, 11, 14, 96–97; origins of, 26–29; philosophical

# Back Issue/Subscription Order Form

Copy or detach and send to:
**Jossey-Bass Inc., Publishers, 350 Sansome Street, San Francisco CA 94104-1342**

Call or fax toll free!
**Phone 888-378-2537 6AM-5PM PST; Fax 800-605-2665**

Back issues:    Please send me the following issues at $23 each.
(Important: please include series initials and issue number, such as EV90.)

1. EV _____

_____

_____

$ _____ Total for single issues

$ _____ Shipping charges (for single issues *only;* subscriptions are exempt
from shipping charges): Up to $30, add $5$^{50}$ • $30$^{01}$–$50, add $6$^{50}$
$50$^{01}$–$75, add $7$^{50}$ • $75$^{01}$–$100, add $9 • $100$^{01}$–$150, add $10
Over $150, call for shipping charge.

Subscriptions    Please ❏ start   ❏ renew my subscription to *New Directions
for Evaluation* for the year 19___ at the following rate:

❏ Individual $65      ❏ Institutional $115
**NOTE:** Subscriptions are quarterly, and are for the calendar year only.
Subscriptions begin with the spring issue of the year indicated above.
For shipping outside the U.S., please add $25.

$ _____ Total single issues and subscriptions (CA, IN, NJ, NY and DC
residents, add sales tax for single issues. NY and DC residents must
include shipping charges when calculating sales tax. NY and Canadian
residents only, add sales tax for subscriptions.)

❏ Payment enclosed (U.S. check or money order only)
❏ VISA, MC, AmEx, Discover Card #_____ Exp. date_____

Signature _____ Day phone _____
❏ Bill me (U.S. institutional orders only. Purchase order required.)
Purchase order #_____

Name _____
Address _____

_____

Phone_____ E-mail _____

For more information about Jossey-Bass Publishers, visit our Web site at:
www.josseybass.com                    **PRIORITY CODE = ND1**

OTHER TITLES AVAILABLE IN THE
NEW DIRECTIONS FOR EVALUATION SERIES
*Jennifer C. Greene, Gary T. Henry,* Coeditors-in-Chief